ARE YOU AN UNDEREARNER?

- Are you usually in debt?
- Do you have little money in savings, and few assets?
- Are you often in financial crisis?
- Do you often feel stress, pain, and fear over money?
- Do you do a lot of unpaid work: volunteer, charity, or showcase work?
- Do you have only a vague idea what your expenses are?
- Do you make do with clothes and possessions that are old, worn out, or insufficient?
- Are you certain *something* will come along to ease your financial situation?
- Do you fear spending money and feel resentful when you must—but sometimes go on buying binges?
- Do you believe that money would solve all your problems?

These are some of the characteristics of underearners. If you answered yes to many of these questions—and are ready to change the way in which you relate to money—you will find here the practical help and empowerment you need, from someone who has conquered underearning in his own life.

Jerrold Mundis
EARN WHAT YOU DESERVE

EARN WHAT YOU DESERVE

HOW TO STOP UNDEREARNING

&

START THRIVING

Jerrold Mundis

Bantam Books

New York Toronto London Sydney Auckland

This, with love, is for Joanna
and for Sarah

and for many others
whom I have met and come
to care for over the past decade

EARN WHAT YOU DESERVE
PUBLISHING HISTORY
Bantam hardcover edition / February 1995
Bantam paperback edition / March 1996

ISBN 0-553-57222-9

Published simultaneously in the United States and Canada

Bantam Books are published by Bantam Books, a division of Random House, Inc. Its
trademark, consisting of the words "Bantam Books" and the portrayal of a rooster, is
Registered in U.S. Patent and Trademark Office and in other countries. Marca Registrada.
Bantam Books, 1540 Broadway, New York, New York 10036.

PRINTED IN THE UNITED STATES OF AMERICA
OPM 10 9 8 7 6 5 4 3

CONTENTS

PREFACE

THIS IS A BOOK ABOUT PROSPERING, ABOUT CEASING TO UNDER-
earn—forever.

You, like me, like every other American, either:

1. Have trouble meeting your bills
2. Can manage them, but never seem able to
   create savings
3. Or you have a surplus of money and rarely feel
   uncomfortable about how much you earn or
   save

Most of us fall into the first or second of these groups.
And of those, millions of us do for no *apparent* reason—and
despite our best efforts not to.

If *you* are such a person, as I am, then this book is for you.

In my first book on personal money, *How to Get Out of
Debt, Stay Out of Debt & Live Prosperously*, I shared my own experience (and that of others) with getting free of debt and pre-

sented a comprehensive program, called Back to the Black, that has since helped tens of thousands of people free themselves from debt.

This book, *Earn What You Deserve*, is the next logical step. It will teach you step by step how to liberate yourself from underearning, stay free of it forever, and live a life of prosperity and abundance from then on. It will do this whether you're already out of debt or still getting out, whether you are an underearner who's never had much trouble with debt, or someone who simply feels that you haven't been earning the kind of money you might be. Even if the question of underearning is completely irrelevant to you, and you perceive yourself just to be in a money or career rut, you'll still find valuable material here that will help you manage your money more effectively, bring more of it in, and use it in more pleasurable ways.

HARK, ARE THOSE THE FOOTFALLS OF A MESSENGER?

"Pain is the messenger," a man named Walter used to say.

I first heard him say that more than a decade ago. I didn't know what he meant then. I do now.

Pain is the messenger: *It tells me that something is wrong.*

I trip, feel pain in my leg. I look down and see a piece of bone sticking through the skin—my leg is broken. Pain, the messenger, is telling me that something is wrong, that I am hurt, that I need to do something to help myself. Without the pain, I wouldn't know anything was wrong. I'd injure myself further.

Emotional or psychological pain, or discomfort, works the same way. It brings me a message: Something is wrong, you need to do something, to *change* something.

Three years ago, I was in pain. It was a kind of pain I had

experienced before. But I hadn't known earlier what was wrong, what I needed to do, and didn't know then, either. I was bottoming-out again financially. I had been solvent—meaning, for our purposes, that I hadn't incurred any new debt—for six years, and had paid off much of my old debt, and my life had certainly gotten better for that. But now, for the fourth time since I had begun to get free of debt and debting, I was running out of money—again.

I knew I'd get through, that because I was committed to not incurring any new debt, was willing to go to any lengths not to, I would find a way. Still, I was weary and discouraged. But I had no name for what was wrong, and so couldn't even begin to imagine how to make it better. One afternoon I was expressing my disaffection to a friend, Jim Roi, a philosopher and a counselor. Jim said to me, sensitively:

"Jerry do you think—is it possible—could it be—that you are a compulsive underearner?"

I found the thought repulsive (whatever it might mean) and rejected it out of hand. Who wouldn't?

But two weeks later, after strenuous internal protest, and some frightening and disturbing thought, I knew what I was: I was, I *am*, a compulsive underearner.

(Don't be alarmed by the word *compulsive* here. That's me. There are other kinds of underearners, too, and we'll be talking about them all in Chapter 1.)

And thus this book. It is the first, to my knowledge, ever written on underearning. It defines the condition, describes its characteristics, and sets out a complete program of liberation —called Prospering.

THIS ISN'T ABOUT WORKING HARDER OR LIVING ON
CHICKEN WINGS

It's about ceasing to underearn, forever—no matter how long you've been doing it, no matter how hard you might have tried to overcome it before.

It's not about working overtime or at a job you hate. It's not a get-rich scheme or a system of austerity.

It's Prospering—a clear and simple program that will enable you to free yourself from underearning, to stay free forever, and to bring abundance into your life.

Sure. Uh-huh.

Be as skeptical as you want. If you follow this program, you'll still free yourself from underearning. These are not simply theoretical ideas. They've been tested and proven over the last three years by a large number of men and women who have already used them to free themselves from underearning; many more are using them right now to do the same thing. You can too.

This program works. It's that simple.

YOU ARE NOT ALONE

Underearning is a term that makes most of us draw back uneasily. It is embarrassing, unpleasant. We feel that anyone who might be affected by it—whatever it is—might somehow be defective or incapable.

Yet underearning is *rampant* in America.

It's not possible to say just how many Americans are underearning at some level or another, and experiencing pain or distress because of it. The condition has never been quantified, no surveys done. But it *is* possible to make an educated guess.

Given the number of people who are overwhelmed by debt or living under pressure because of it—nearly 50 million—and given my personal and professional work in the field of debt recovery, earning, and other areas of personal money over the past decade, I'd estimate the number to be somewhere between 20 and 30 million.

Underearning cuts across all social and occupational strata —from doctors and lawyers to carpenters and teachers, from psychologists and executives to house painters and waitresses, from consultants and secretaries to stock clerks and stockbrokers.

You are not alone in this.

Some of us, though a minority, are earning an income that may appear at first to rule out the possibility of underearning —$100,000, even more. (How that's possible will be discussed in Chapter 1.) At the opposite pole, others of us are on unemployment. Most lie somewhere in between. Some of us owe tens of thousands of dollars, others no more than $500 or $1,000, or even nothing at all. But underearning is underearning, no matter the form, and sooner or later it can—and frequently does—poison our lives.

WHAT UNDEREARNING DOES TO US

In time, underearning grinds down our spirit and our hopes. It exhausts us. It sucks the joy and pleasure out of our days. We come to live in fear that we're going to run out of money, that we won't have enough for the rent, the mortgage, our own tuition or our children's; that we'll be caught in a squeeze, hauled into court, end up as a bag lady.

This fear begins to disrupt our lives and personal relationships. The emotional and physical toll it takes can be enormous. We can come to feel defeated and hopeless; depressed; live in anxiety and despair. We may experience pain, perhaps even impulses toward suicide. The quality of our entire lives is eroded.

Underearning, regardless of the level of discomfort it causes, is an unpleasant condition for anyone. It is also wholly unnecessary.

WHERE THIS PROGRAM COMES FROM

Prospering evolved out of nearly a decade of not-debting for me, the last three years of which I spent consciously and actively working to remedy my own underearning. During this period, I had the opportunity to observe firsthand a large number of people in support groups and in the workshops and seminars I led on debt and money across the country who were also, I believe, underearners. Many of them have since come to identify themselves as such, and some I have worked closely with.

Some of the concepts, techniques, and strategies in Prospering originated in Debtors Anonymous (though this book is in no way connected with that organization, which as policy neither supports nor opposes any outside projects).* Other material comes from individual members of DA, from complementary sources such as consciousness seminars, metaphysical disciplines, and prosperity workshops, and still more I have conceptualized and formulated specifically for this purpose.

---

* Debtors Anonymous (DA) is a self-help organization that was founded in 1976. It has grown rapidly and now has chapters in many areas of the United States and in several foreign countries. The only requirement for membership is a desire to stop incurring debt. DA is wholly self-supporting through the voluntary contributions of its members, whose primary purpose is to remain solvent and to help other people in debt to achieve solvency.

In the end, all of it has been filtered through my own personal experience and evolves out of my close contact with the many men and women from all walks of life who have already liberated themselves from the pain and stress of underearning, and the many more who are doing so now.

From my own experience and theirs, I can tell you that not only is freedom from underearning possible, but that it will always materialize if we work for it. I have seen people increase their incomes substantially, even double and triple them. I have seen myself make more money than ever I did in any other three-year period of my life. I have seen people who had scarcely been supporting themselves come to do so comfortably and happily. Most important, though, I and they have won a growing psychological and emotional freedom from the stress and pain of underearning, of never having quite enough on which to live humanely, or of breaking free only to return to that terrible point, again and again.

Those days are gone for me now. I live mostly in peace with money. I can buy all that I need and many things I want. I take vacations, have savings. Did I get rich? No. In time, I may—or may not. But I do today, right now, live prosperously and abundantly.

With this program, if you choose, you too can do what I and others have done.

YOU DON'T HAVE TO UNDEREARN ANYMORE

Sure I don't. And your mother wears combat boots.

But it's true. It has been true for me; it has been true for a great many others. It is true for you.

I am not telling you that the sky's the limit or that you

can be, do, or have anything you want. It isn't, and you can't. But I *am* telling you that you can free yourself from underearning and stay free of it forever: by using the program in this book, which is a clear, simple, and step-by-step guide.

All you need to do is to begin reading.

PART I
BEGINNING

1.

IN ALL ITS GLORY

IN THIS CHAPTER, WE'RE GOING TO DEFINE UNDEREARNING, discuss its dynamics, and give an overview of Prospering. First, though, I'd like to amplify slightly on how this book came to be written, to establish a context.

A ROAD WELL TRAVELED

I first heard Walter say that pain is the messenger in a roomful of people who didn't drink or take drugs. There was something else Walter used to say: "The lesson will be repeated—until it's learned."

Both these statements have proved true for me, and valuable; I think they are true for everyone.

Over the next seven years, my life got progressively better. I worked to make it better. When pain came, I listened; I found ways to change, different ways to do things. The first major change I had made was to cease using chemical mood-changers myself. I undertook the next one a year later. I was in terrible, constant pain over my debts, which seemed to me almost insurmountable then. Someone introduced me to a support group for people in debt, and from that day on, one day at a time, I did not incur another new debt in any form.*

And my life got better.

Still, something was wrong. Fundamentally wrong, though at first that was not apparent to me.

I didn't debt, but I kept bottoming-out—running out of money. Each time, I watched the operating fund I had managed to build being depleted, drained away despite all my efforts to prevent that, until there was nothing left. Until I had no money at all. None. The pain, and fear, were excruciating.

I would not debt, was willing to go to any length not to. There was a time when that willingness meant not buying Christmas presents for my sons—a difficult and humbling thing to do. There were times when it meant pulling up the couch cushions and going through my jacket pockets looking for change so I could buy food over the weekend for myself and my youngest son, whom I had down from the country every other weekend.

Being solvent—not incurring any new debt, one day at a time—wasn't always so grim. I paid off many thousands of dollars of debt during those years, bought clothes, and took vacations. But sooner or later (without being a profligate spender), I would bottom-out once more, get down to zero, have no money left—no matter how hard I worked, what I tried.

I am not lazy. I am not unintelligent. Nor untalented or incapable. And I was willing to do whatever was necessary to

---

* By this, I mean *unsecured* debt. For a discussion of the difference between secured and unsecured debt, and why that difference is important to people who are working to get out of debt, see Appendix A.

free myself from debt and debting. Why, then, did I keep ending up like this?

I think during those years that I somehow always sensed there was another, perhaps even more powerful issue behind debting for me (or one at least *as* powerful). In meetings focused on recovery from debt I sometimes attended, most people identified themselves as debtors when they spoke: "Hi, I'm Bob, and I'm a debtor." I didn't. Certainly I *was* a debtor (someone who'd had repeated trouble with debt), but I felt that to call myself such would be vaguely inaccurate, somehow insufficient, perhaps even self-misleading. So what I would say was, "Hi, I'm Jerry. I have a long history of incurring debt."

Which was the truth, but which also kept the question open.

Still, there was a pattern here—*something* was happening, kept happening, that returned me to the very edge of debting, to lack and deprivation again.

So now, after much thought, I named *self-created lack* as something with which I had a terrible problem, over which I was powerless, and that was making my life unmanageable. I hoped that by perceiving it thus and by taking appropriate actions (as I had with not-debting), I could begin to free myself from it, too. (This is a tricky concept, which we'll discuss fully in Chapters 3 and 9.)

For a while, I tried working with the concept of self-created lack. In the end, it wasn't right. It was *approaching* what I needed to find, but wasn't the thing itself. With regret, I stopped working with the idea. That was not the right name.

I knew something was wrong. But what was it?

And that's where I was when Jim Roi said to me: "Jerry, do you think—is it possible—could it be—that you are a compulsive underearner?"

• • •

Over the years I had heard an occasional person in debt recovery refer to himself or herself as an underearner, or temporary underearner, or even—though rarely—compulsive underearner. But no one had ever defined just what that might mean or addressed how one might go about freeing oneself from it.

I am a compulsive underearner.

Has a kind of frightening, final ring to it, doesn't it?

Bless you, my child. (And thank God I'm not one, whatever it means!)

Even the simple *I am an underearner*, without that brutal modifier, is distasteful to most people.

No wonder no one has wanted to touch the issue. But the paradox is that that very admission—"I am an underearner"—makes liberation possible, makes it unnecessary, one day at a time, to continue underearning.

This time when I began to work with the concept, naming myself a compulsive underearner, the impact was immediate and enormous. I knew I had found the right name at last.

UNDEREARNING: WHAT IT IS

All right. So what *is* underearning?

To *earn*, in its primary dictionary sense, means to gain salary, wages, or other reward for your service, labor, or performance. To earn, then, is to gain income from what you do.

So, then:

To *underearn* is repeatedly to gain less income than you need, or than would be beneficial—usually for no apparent reason, and despite your desire to do otherwise.

What do we mean by *need*? And by *less than would be beneficial*?

We are defining *need* here in its most basic sense: an amount that is enough for you to provide yourself with food, shelter, and clothing of decent quality on a regular basis.

That's the amount of income you *need*.

While owning a co-op on the park, buying a new car every year, or having the money to pay for your daughter's medical education at Stanford might be pleasurable and even desirable, they are not needs.

Beneficial is more open to interpretation. For our purposes, it means enough for you to meet your basic needs, with some left over to spend on items or quality that exceed those needs, a bit more for recreation or relaxation, and some to put into savings. As a threshold definition, that is what we mean by *beneficial*.

Underearning is *not* synonymous with having a low income, though it often involves one. Many people earn a low income who are not underearners. They bring in more than they need to cover their basic expenses, and provide themselves with some pleasure and savings, and they display few of the characteristics common to underearners. (These are discussed in the next chapter.)

Nor is *underearning* synonymous with *underachieving*. People can achieve less, even a great deal less, than their potential and still earn more than they need or than is basically beneficial to them.

Nor, finally, is *underearning* synonymous with *underworking*. Most underearners, on the contrary, work very hard. They simply make sure, in some way, that what they get back from their effort is either not enough or just marginally enough to get by on.

So low levels of income achievement, or work—or simply levels lower than one is capable of—while frequently associated with underearning, are not in themselves indicators of underearning.

What, then, *are*?

Underearning is a self-diagnosed condition—and needs to be. No underearner will ever get free of underearning without first perceiving, or accepting, that he or she *is* an underearner. Not hearing it from someone else, but perceiving it for *himself, herself*. Surely, it is sometimes objected, not everyone who has ever had trouble bringing in enough money to meet his needs is an underearner? No, of course not. Just as not everyone who has ever been drunk is an alcoholic.

Chapter 2 contains detailed discussions of the most common indicators of a difficulty with underearning. Use them to determine how serious your own situation with underearning may or may not be.

Is underearning an illness of some sort? It may be, it may not. Certainly it's not a physical illness, but the argument can be made that underearning, like other self-damaging behaviors, is a psychological and spiritual illness. (We'll deal with those aspects as we go along.) But ultimately—is it? For some, it probably is; for others, it isn't. But *what* it is, is less important than *that* it is. There is a *condition* of underearning, a *state* of underearning, an *ontology* of underearning. So whatever it may or may not actually be, it is perfectly fine, I think, to call it an illness, a malady, an affliction, a habit, tendency, mindset, or anything else you might wish.

Whatever underearning may ultimately be, there are basically three kinds of it: Compulsive, Problematic, and Minor.

Compulsive Underearning

Throw out all the psychological jargon you've heard about compulsion. Basically, a compulsion is simply an act that is repeated over and over. It is motivated by an internal reason or set of reasons, usually subconscious. Some compulsions are harmless, such as arranging pens on a desk or cans on a shelf in a certain order. Generally we think of them as no more than habits or personal preference, if we think of them at all.

When a compulsion is harmful—serious drinking or over-eating, for example—we try to deny that it's a compulsion. We manufacture excuses for it: "Hey, I work hard, and I need a couple of drinks to unwind." We minimize its destructive consequences: "So I'm carrying a few pounds too much. It's no big deal, I'll knock 'em off by summer." We even claim that the consequences of our behavior are actually the cause of the behavior: "I borrow money because my life is pressured, hard, and painful"—when in fact life has become pressured, hard, and painful because of our borrowing or not paying bills, which follow the underearning.

Compulsive underearning is repeatedly to gain less income than you need, or than would be beneficial, *despite the negative emotional and practical consequences that follow.* And it is to do so in the face of your conscious efforts or desire to do otherwise. It is to be, in effect, *powerless* over the repeated act of bringing in less than you need or than would be beneficial.

Which isn't nearly as bad as it might sound at first (and certainly did to me).

Problem Underearning

The difference between problem underearning and compulsive underearning is largely one of scale and intensity. A problem underearner, for example, might underearn only periodically, and generally doesn't experience financial trouble and emotional pain as severely as the compulsive underearner.

Yet.

Some people go into problem underearning because of a temporary situation, such as a career difficulty, or a setback in the economy, or because they don't realize at first just how trying their situation is becoming. When they do realize it, either they're able to change the circumstances or they recognize the direction in which they've begun to drift and bring their underearning to a halt.

For other people, problem underearning is simply compulsive underearning in the making. Underearning is often a progressive condition, building slowly, layer by layer.

In my own case, it was twenty years in the making.

Minor Underearning

Minor underearning is underearning that's almost irrelevant. It's akin to having a mild cold, something you hardly notice, that doesn't bother you much. But the very fact that you've picked up this book means your underearning probably isn't minor. You *have* noticed the problem and *are* bothered by it.

A minor underearner brings in enough income to meet her needs, at least most of the time, often with enough left over for a pleasantry or two, or even to build some savings. What, then, distinguishes her from someone who simply has a low income? Two elements, *in combination*. First, the potential to bring in more. Second, that to do so would be *significantly* beneficial, would mean, for example, being able to buy a house, or have an investment portfolio, or simply take more appealing vacations. Most likely, the minor underearner in your life is your brother, your spouse, or a good friend rather than you.

But that is not always the case. It's possible that it *is* you —just beginning to awake to that fact, just beginning to feel dissatisfied. Perhaps you are recognizing that you could do more, want to, and wonder why that has not been happening.

ITS TWO ASPECTS

Underearning—whether compulsive, problematic, or minor—has two aspects, though they occasionally blur. (Making this distinction is helpful in seeing underearning, but don't worry about being precise.) They are: *active* underearning and *passive* underearning.

Active Underearning

Active underearning involves *doing something* that results in underearning, from quitting a job, to setting low fees, to turning down work. For example:

- Seeking work for which you're not qualified
- Making unreasonable demands on an employer or client
- Spending time on projects or activities that will make little or no money
- Incurring heavy expenses
- Botching a job
- Telling prospective clients or employers that you don't know how to do what they want to hire you for
- Behaving obnoxiously or offensively on the job or with clients
- Accepting work you know will pay you less than you need
- Making promises you can't fulfill
- Exhausting yourself during nonworking hours
- Investing more time on a job than you're being paid to invest

What follows, which comes from my own life, is a classic example of active underearning: I wrote most of my books under pseudonyms. Whenever one of those pseudonyms became famous, built a loyal readership, I killed that name and began writing under a new one.

I had "conscious" reasons for doing this—an elitist, Flaubertian attitude about the difference between art and commerce; the fact that readers want a writer to produce the same kind of book each time (if he's a historical novelist, they don't want to see him write a mystery); the fact that publishing houses want an exclusive on a writer and don't want him writing for other houses. There were other reasons, too, and there was some truth in all of them. But the real truth—though I didn't know it then—was that changing names was a near-perfect function of my compulsion to underearn. It is difficult even in the best of circumstances to establish a reputation and make a living as a writer in the United States; I put myself through the additional trial of having to do it three separate times, under three different names.

Sonya is another example of active underearning. A dental hygienist in Cleveland, Sonya spent more money on her son than she could afford, trying to compensate for a divorce that had deprived the boy of his father's presence. As a result, she had a difficult time nearly every month trying to meet the rent. She tended to quarrel with the dentists for whom she worked, feeling exploited by them, and had worked in six different offices in the previous ten years. She had been fired from each and had spent months without income, during which she had fallen into debt, before she could find another job. Finally she decided to leave the field and tried for two years to get a job as a paralegal, an area in which she had no experience. By these actions, Sonya was actively underearning.

Passive Underearning

Passive underearning involves *not doing* or *failing to do something* that would—if you did it—cause you to earn more. It can be anything from not getting to work on time to failing to meet a deadline or neglecting to ask for help or advice. Passive underearning is more subtle than active underearning and may be more difficult to discern at first, yet there are probably as many ways to do it as there are to actively underearn. For example:

- Ignoring or blinding yourself to an opportunity
- Failing to request a raise
- Not knowing what your expenses are
- Not attempting something unless you're positive it will work
- Failing to fulfill responsibilities
- Not increasing fees
- Not making sales calls
- Waiting for something to happen that will make things better
- Not capitalizing on skills or abilities
- Failing to wonder if there's anything you could do to make more money
- Not drawing up a business or personal career plan
- Feeling that everything results from fate, that there's nothing you can do to change it, and failing truly to test that belief

Here's an example of passive underearning from my own life.

As a consultant, I break writer's block for people. Forever, in one four-hour consultation. For a long time, I did this strictly by referral, by word of mouth. If you happened to run into someone who happened to know me, and if that person happened to tell you about me, and if you got my phone number, and if I happened to be home when you called, or felt I could make myself available, then I would probably do it for you.

When someone suggested to me that this was a valuable and probably widely desired service, that it could be a good source of income for me, and that I should advertise, it took me more than a year to bring myself to the point of being able to do that. I could not bear the thought of advertising, of putting my name and telephone number in print, of having people call me personally and having to sell myself over the phone. Finally I did—and the response was quite positive. But even then, it took me three years to raise my rates from where they were when I began to where they are now, which is nearly four times the original amount.

Gary, a bright man in his early forties, had a history of debting and a checkered working life—long periods of low income punctuated with occasional periods of high income. When I met him, he had been living in lack for several years. Most recently having worked in part-time jobs and as an office temp, he was drawing unemployment and was scarcely able to meet his basic expenses. When a friend set him up for a nearly guaranteed job with a bookstore, Gary didn't even make the phone call. "I probably wouldn't make any more there than I'm getting from unemployment," he said. "And if I took the job, I wouldn't be available for something better." He might have been right. It might *not* have made sense for him to take the job. But the point is, he didn't even make the call to find out. That is passive underearning.

It's possible you've been growing uncomfortable as you've been reading this chapter, or even experiencing a strong negative reaction. You might want to roar out denial, or, just the opposite, be tempted to think that your underearning is hopeless. If so, don't worry. These are perfectly natural reactions. Who wouldn't be upset when first encountering the possibility that he or she might be an underearner?

Me, I found it repulsive. When finally I did begin to consider it, I went sliding toward despair. And later, when I sat down to write out a history of my earning—or underearning—so I could see it in black and white, and decide what was real and what wasn't, I became sick to my stomach at the prospect.

The good news is, these are the first small steps on the road to liberation: One day at a time, you don't have to underearn anymore.

UNDEREARNING IS ABOUT MONEY—NOT ABOUT LOVE, ART, FAME, GLORY, OR PERSONAL RELATIONSHIPS

Underearning has to do with money, not with abstractions, emotions, or anything else. With money—with repeatedly bringing in less of it than you need. Underearning does not involve bringing in less love than you need. Or getting less recreation than you need. Or not spending enough time on your art. Or anything else. Those may all be valid issues related to underearning, be part of a *syndrome* around underearning, but they are not underearning itself.

There is a danger, in the first flush of discovery, or early stages of healing, of trying to extend the concept of underearning so that it becomes all-embracing. This only confuses the issue and makes remedying the problem much more difficult, if not impossible. In some support groups focused on recovery from debt, some people began to call themselves self-debtors, emotional debtors, and the like. At its extreme, people were speaking of time-debting, play-debting, art-debting, and even space-debting (not having enough room). This hopelessly confused the real problem for them. Even worse, it confused the people who were coming into those groups for the first time, under terrible pressure from their debts and trying to find help. The practice led to such irrational statements as, "I'm not going to debt to myself anymore, so I borrowed three hundred dollars from my brother to buy a new winter coat." In that statement the entire concept of not incurring any new unsecured debt one day at a time, of *recovering* from debt, is lost.

There are many issues *related* to the problem of underearning, but they are not the problem itself. The beginning of wisdom, goes an old Chinese epigram, is to call things by their right name. To underearn is to gain less *money* than you need. Other issues, which either contribute to underearning or result from it, are part of the *syndrome* of underearning.

WHERE IT COMES FROM

Where does underearning come from?

The stars. Childhood. Metabolism. Past lives.

Who knows?

Freudians might have one argument; psychopharmacologists another. People steeped in ACOA theory (Adult Children of Alcoholics) would be quite certain they knew, as would astrologers, who would dismiss the ACOAs. Cognitive and rational-emotive therapists would dismiss the Freudians, the ACOAs, and the astrologers. Trance-channelers would have a different opinion altogether. So would New Age thinkers. And that is not even to begin to mention the others, like sociologists, multi-culturalists, the Pope, or your mother.

There is probably some truth in everyone's idea, and more in ideas unsuspected yet. However, *how* I got hurt is less important than that I *am* hurt. If I get up in the middle of the night for a glass of water, don't turn on the light, slip on an ice cube I dropped earlier, fall over a misplaced chair, and break my leg—my problem is a broken leg, not how I broke it. In fact, knowing precisely how I broke it, the exact sequence that led to the injury, is not going to help me one bit. My need, first, is to understand that my leg is broken, and second, to take action to get it repaired.

Self-knowledge is always desirable, and often useful. But rarely in itself has it been able to stop or alter self-damaging behavior, especially when that behavior has become compulsive or near compulsive. No analysis ever got a drinker to stop drinking or a binger to stop eating, no matter how thoroughly her past was explored or how deeply his unconscious was plumbed. Such work can be very helpful, but usually when done as an adjunct to a program of change, such as those based on or similar to the self-help, Twelve Step model. Once recuperation is under way, then to become more familiar with your own internal nature—whether through analytic therapy, deep meditation, or whatever other means is effective for you —can only be beneficial.

I have watched people who had a problem with debt or underearning crying "But my childhood, my childhood . . . ," obsessed with how they *got* the way they were (or thought they did) rather than trying to *deal with* the way they were. I never saw any of them get better. Clearly, everyone was influenced by his or her childhood, and later we'll be working with techniques that take that into account. But how we got the way we are—even if we could know that for certain —isn't as important as what we do about the way we are.

"Moondust, the Smell of Hay, and Dialectical Materialism": that was the title of a short story written many years ago by an old friend when we were young writers together in the city. The three elements represented the essence of the main character, a marooned cosmonaut. All three had brought him to the moment in which he found himself. And that is where your underearning comes from, from all the elements that have contributed to forming the essence of who you are. The question is: What now?

SO WHAT DO WE DO ABOUT IT?

The first step in freeing yourself from underearning is to accept responsibility for the problem. This doesn't mean it is your fault. The fact that you are an underearner, if you are, is not a condition you wanted or that you brought upon yourself. You may be completely justified in thinking that you were neglected or terribly abused somehow as a child, and yes, it may truly be a shame, and yes, perhaps anyone would empathize with you. But going over that repeatedly is not going to help you free yourself—no one ever got better confessing someone else's sins.

That you are an underearner, while not your fault, *is* your responsibility. What you do about it is your responsibility. No one can change that for you; no external event or circumstance will alter it. But by accepting that it is your responsibility, you can begin to free yourself from ever having to underearn again.

Prospering, the basic program of liberation from underearning presented in this book, has three main elements: (1) practical techniques and actions; (2) spiritual or psychological techniques and actions; and (3) the Twelve Steps.* The first of these, the practical techniques and actions, are discussed beginning in Chapter 3.

In Chapter 2, we'll discuss the identifying characteristics of underearners, in order to get a better understanding of the condition.

---

* A set of nonsectarian spiritual principles discussed in Part IV.

2.

UNDEREARNERS

WHAT FOLLOW ARE THE MOST COMMON CHARACTERISTICS THAT indicate a problem with underearning. There are nineteen of them. Not every underearner will display them all, and anyone might evidence one or two, or even several, without being an underearner; in fact, many people who aren't underearners do. But *any person who exhibits most of them, or a majority of them, probably is an underearner*—and someone likely to be headed toward increasing pain and difficulty unless he or she recognizes the problem and begins to take steps to correct it.

Remember as you read this chapter that finding yourself here more often than not—if you do—should be a source not of distress but of relief. To recognize and admit the problem is the first step in liberating yourself from it, toward a life that is happy, joyous, and free. Here, then, are the characteristics most often demonstrated by underearners, and in the most common ways.

CHARACTERISTICS

1. Underearners Are Usually in Debt.

You are in debt. (Unsecured debt; secured debt is not relevant here.) Maybe for tens of thousands of dollars, maybe for no more than a hundred. Your debt may be to a bank or to a friend. It may be credit card or department store debt. It may be back taxes you owe. It could be that you're a month behind in your rent, or that you owe money to your dentist or therapist. Or simply that you're habitually late paying your phone bill or other bills, resulting in a past-due balance. All these are debts—money you owe. The amount is not important—what is, is that you *are* in debt. Debt is debt, whether it's for five dollars or fifty thousand.

But hey, everybody puts a dinner on a credit card, bounces a check, or borrows a couple of bucks now and then, don't they?

No, not everybody. Quite a few, yes, but not everybody.

What's significant here is that *you* are in debt, and *perpetually* so. You still haven't paid off your student loan. There's always a balance on your credit card. You rarely get your bills mailed out on time. You are never *out* of debt, and you haven't been for years, month after month. In fact, it's probably hard for you to remember the last time you didn't owe something to somebody.

People go into debt for reasons not necessarily related to underearning, of course. These range from a setback in a career to an upheaval in the economy, from not understanding basic personal finance to using money as a mood-changer. But the fact remains that the majority of underearners *are* in debt in some amount or another.

It is sometimes thought, and logically, that a high or above-average income is proof against underearning. And often it is. However, while most underearners do bring in a modest or low income, that is not always true.

Ken, who fixes outboard motors and snowmobiles in northern Wisconsin, makes $27,000 a year. He's carrying little unsecured debt, doesn't feel any special pain or pressure over his finances, and he and his family are generally happy with their lives. Ken is not an underearner. Valerie, a performance artist who lives in New York, makes $75,000 a year, most of which goes to expenses of various kinds: travel, wardrobe, materials. She is in debt and experiences frequent stress about money. Valerie is an underearner.

Ken does not repeatedly bring in less money than he needs or than would be beneficial to him. Valerie, despite the negative emotional and practical consequences that follow, does.*

It's also possible to be a solvent debtor—one who's correcting his situation, who isn't incurring any new debt and is liquidating old ones—and still to suffer from underearning. This was true in my case. For six years, I didn't incur debt, and in that span experienced substantial recovery. But still I kept bottoming-out, not knowing how or why, until finally I was able to recognize myself as an underearner. I am definitely a debtor; I have a serious problem with debt. But for me, underearning is the malady *behind* debting. It is the primary *cause* of my debting. This is true of a great many other debtors, too, both solvent and not.

It is true of Mary, a civil servant in Chicago who had not incurred any new debt in five years but was never able to get more than a week or two weeks' expenses ahead in savings. It is true of Robert and his wife, who live in Boston, she a social

* It could be argued that Valerie's problem is overspending or even compulsive spending. In another case, that might be true. But Valerie—and other high-income underearners like her—cannot generate the income she does, doing what she does, without these expenses. That is the key: An overspender *could* reduce her expenditures considerably if she were so inclined, without reducing the size of her income at all.

worker, he a pioneering software writer who once, unexpectedly, made a great deal of money, watched it drain away over several years, then lived in painful, near poverty for the next decade. And it is true of Chuck, an intelligent, multitalented psychotherapist in Atlanta who, though he lives modestly, cannot afford to take his wife and children away for a week's vacation and who defaulted on a student loan because he couldn't meet the payment schedule. There are endless others.

A form of denial that can rise up here is the belief that since you don't owe *much* money, it's not really debt. Or not recognizing that failing to pay your rent in the month it's due, or a bill by its due date, or taking services such as dental work without paying for them when you receive them, are all forms of debt.

Among underearners who *aren't* in debt, those most often in denial are the ones being supported by their families (such as adult children from wealthy backgrounds) or by social organizations (such as clerics or people frequently drawing unemployment or social assistance), or who are living partly on grants and stipends and spend much of their time applying for more of them.

2. Underearners Have Little Savings, Few Assets.

You have hardly any savings and no operating fund. One serious hit—losing your job, a fire, a medical emergency—would wipe you out. Month by month, practically every dollar you get in goes right back out. (As a rule of thumb, most people need at least three months' total living expenses set aside in a contingency fund. This is a safety net, to cover them in case of emergency or difficult, unforeseen circumstances. Self-employed people need at least six months' expenses.)

You have few assets, if any. You have no investment portfolio, don't own works of art or other pieces of property such as jewelry that you could sell for cash or use to collateralize a loan if you needed money. You probably rent your quarters. If you *do* own your dwelling—house, co-op, or condominium—then it's likely to be your only asset. And you probably came into it out of good fortune—through a settlement, inheritance, or being a statutory tenant when the building went co-op—rather than by buying it on the open market. If you did buy it on the open market, you may well have borrowed some of the down payment from a relative or friend. If you somehow managed to build up equity in it over the years, you've probably already taken out a second mortgage on it.

3. Underearners Are Often in Financial Crisis.

Everyone gets into a financial crisis now and then. It's nearly impossible not to. But underearners do it all the time.

You're often short of cash, frequently have to scramble to borrow money or find extra work on an emergency basis. You know what past-due notices look like. Creditors may be dunning you, threatening legal action. You're usually only a paycheck or two ahead of catastrophe, of falling off the financial tightrope, of not being able to pay your bills or even of meeting your basic needs.

Sometimes you rush to the bank to deposit your paycheck, commission check, or other income check (even borrowed money), fearful that it might not clear in time to cover the checks you have to write immediately or that you've already written. Paula, an acting coach in debt recovery, was endlessly making trips to the bank to deposit one small check after another from her students. Often, on the final day or two of the month, she had to rush across town between appointments in order to get her rent in at the last possible moment. Once she was too embarrassed to appear at the realty office in person, since this was the third month in a row she had been this late, so she spent twelve dollars to hire a messenger to deliver it.

If a check you've deposited is returned as unpayable because of insufficient funds, you grow incensed—because your own finances are so precarious that even the slightest misstep can tip you over the edge into bouncing checks of your own. Your cash reserve account, checking-plus, or privileged checking—whatever your bank calls its overdraft privilege—is always hovering right up near the maximum that can be advanced to you.

It seems that *something* is always happening, something that demands more money than you have: a car repair, computer breakdown, unexpected trip; a root canal, glasses for your oldest child, an insurance premium you forgot about.

4. Underearners Feel Pain, Stress, and Fear Over Money.

Money is a subject that causes intense emotions in you, most of them negative. You feel pain over it, stress, and fear.

You feel *pain* because you rarely have enough money to use for pleasure or play or on holiday. You feel pain from feeling defeated, weary of the struggle just to bring in enough on which to survive. Or from the shame of making or having so little, the belief that you'll always have to work at a job you don't like in order to make ends meet, that the future holds little that doesn't already exist in your present. Or from feeling restricted and inhibited by the lack of money, maybe even from thinking about getting married or having children.

The *stress* you feel results from putting all your energy into work, leaving little for anything else. From your anger: at your parents, at profiteering landlords, the IRS. From feeling hopeless. From feeling you are flawed or incapable.

The *fear* is that you won't be able to pay the rent or take care of yourself or your family. That you'll become dependent on charity. That there will be no place to stay and nothing to eat; that you will die.

Rick, who had once been a corporate speechwriter, became so paralyzed with fear in his bottoming-out on underearning that he could scarcely function in an income-producing way at all. He began his recuperation working as a clerk in a stationery store; he is now the editor of a technical magazine. Sheila, in the final stages of her own bottoming-out, assaulted a co-worker in an outburst of rage at the network studio where she was a video editor. These cases are extreme, but they illustrate clearly the kind of pain, stress, and fear that underearners often come to feel.

5. Underearners Do a Lot of Unpaid Work: Volunteer, Charity, or Showcase Work.

You do a lot of volunteer work at your church, your local recycling center, hospital, animal shelter, or community youth program, or for the March of Dimes. If you belong to a self-help group, you're heavily involved in doing service for it.

You give away the special skills that you have by writing press releases, drawing up posters, sitting on panels, doing carpentry work, painting scenery, putting together music, or organizing logistics. You do this for schools, arts organizations, professional societies, and groups whose causes you support.

As an actor or performer you work for nothing in showcases—in order, you think, to gain publicity, to be seen by people who might want you to work someplace for money, and to get reviews you hope will be useful at some later profit-making date.

You do these things, you believe, because the causes are worthy, because you have been blessed with certain abilities and it's good to give back in return, because giving is an expression of care and loving, because it is your moral obligation to help those in need, because you have the time anyway so why not, because you need the experience, and because it is a wise investment in your future, your career.

All these reasons may in themselves be quite valid—some even highly praiseworthy, and some a real contribution to the betterment of the world or yourself. But when you repeatedly gain less income than you need, this kind of volunteerism, this kind of charity, this kind of showcasing—this expenditure of time, energy, and ability with no income in return—is not truly giving or advancing your career, but simply an act of self-destruction. It is a major function of your underearning.

6. Underearners Often Come from Alcoholic or Otherwise Troubled Families.

You grew up in a household troubled by alcoholism, overeating, codependency, emotional distance, gambling, physical abuse, or some other form of compulsive behavior. Ron, a New York psychotherapist, says he's never seen a problem underearner who did not come from such a background. Karen, a financial counselor in San Francisco who has specialized in working with debtors over the past five years, agrees. By and large I do too, but not completely.

Families troubled by alcoholism or other compulsive behaviors are often called dysfunctional. And indeed, in the original meaning of the word, they are. But *dysfunctional*, unfortunately, is a word that has been greatly overused, even abused, for several years, to the point that it has lost much of its value as a descriptive term. *Dysfunctional* has been employed as a synonym for *murderous, hateful, savage, abusive*, and even *evil*. It is *not* a synonym for any of those.

Dysfunctional means "disordered" or "impaired"; it does not mean "awful," "brutal," or "catastrophic." I suggest, as a practical working definition of a dysfunctional household, this: A dysfunctional household is one in which, because of alcoholism or a similar affliction, the family dynamics are more hurtful or repressive than those in households that are not marked by such an affliction.

To grow up in such a household is certainly unfortunate but not disastrous. Among the possible results are: an uncertain sense of one's self-worth, apprehension, secretiveness, guilt, self-criticism, overreaction, a certain seriousness, and a feeling of detachment. But not all individuals who grow up in dysfunctional families are so affected. Some react in an entirely different way—possibly by way of compensation—and become more confident, bold, and involved, and more loving and open with their own children than they might otherwise have been. My own background can be described as dysfunctional. Yet my brother, who is two years younger than I am, can in no way be considered an underearner; on the contrary, he has been a very high earner nearly from the beginning of his working life. Nor is my sister, who is five years older than I am.

Family income is not significant in forming underearners, either. Some underearners come from impoverished backgrounds, others from privileged and wealthy ones. Most originate from the broad middle.

The majority of severe underearners, however, do come from an alcoholic or otherwise troubled background.

7. Underearners May Resent People with Money.

Some underearners resent people who have more money than they do. This resentment usually stems from envy. They want what others have, but since they don't have it, or think they can't have it, they become angry at those others. A piece of graffiti that sometimes pops up in cities is *Solve Hunger: Eat the*

Rich. Sometimes, more harshly, there's just an angrily scrawled *Eat the Rich!* or even the furious *Kill the Rich!*

Other underearners complain bitterly about people who they think make it difficult or impossible for them to get ahead: an employer, a supervisor, a banker, a lawyer, a politician, even a friend or relative who won't give or lend them money to get through a hard time or start a business or career. But always the complaint is about someone who has more money than they themselves do.

The saddest part about this anger and complaint is that it condemns the underearner to continued underearning. There is an inexorable and self-destructive logic involved in resenting or blaming people who have more money than you do: If they are all corrupt, greedy, and unprincipled, if they are all exploiters and thieves who ought to be taxed out of existence or shot, then how can you possibly ever allow yourself to have money? Because then *you* would be corrupt, greedy, and unprincipled, and *you* ought to be taxed out of existence or shot. You'd have to resent yourself as much as you now resent them.

People who aren't underearners—and some who are—see in those who do have money as merely proof that it's possible to have money and therefore that they themselves have an opportunity to acquire it.

8. Underearners Are Good at Finding Enablers.

An enabler is someone who makes it easier for you to continue to underearn: a relative, friend, business associate, or institution. Your enabler does this by giving or lending you money or allowing you to fall behind in paying a bill. Most enablers are well-meaning. They want to help. But all their gifts, loans, and forbearances do is shield you from the consequences of your underearning a little while longer. You, like most underearners, are very good at finding such people.

Casey, an academic and intellectual in his midthirties with a wife and young child, worked for a kind of think tank most of his working life. This organization was well endowed and supported Casey and the handful of others on permanent staff in generous style for doing research projects of their own choosing and at their own pace. They were routinely advanced money whenever they requested it. Two years ago, when the long-term director was forced to retire and replaced by a younger, more aggressive administrator, policy changed. The staff suddenly found itself held to stricter and more realistic standards. Casey, now being paid for what he produced rather than on some illusionary basis, discovered in a short, painful period that he was an underearner who had been enabled most of his adult life.

In the days when I was still debting I was once so overdue in paying my utility bill that my electricity was shut off. I called the power company. I was a writer, I told them. I worked on an electric typewriter. Without electricity I couldn't write. Without writing I couldn't get paid. Without getting paid I couldn't pay them. Therefore, I needed my electricity turned back on. I successfully talked them into restoring my power that same afternoon, and out of the $150 deposit they had wanted in order to protect themselves against further delinquencies.

It would be helpful here for you to draw up a list of enablers whom you have used yourself over the past year or two. Pause for a moment. Get up and get a note pad. Take a breath, relax. . . .

Now write down the names of all the people and organizations over the past few years who have made it easier for you to continue to underearn by giving or lending you money, extending you credit, or allowing you to fall behind in your bills. These might include banks, finance companies, credit cards, department stores, schools, the government, friends, relatives, acquaintances, your landlord, business associates, doctors, dentists, service providers, and anyone else you can think of.

Do it now.

Have you completed the list? Good. Sit back in your chair and relax. Take a slow, deep breath. Congratulations. In identifying and listing these enablers, you've just taken an important step toward freeing yourself from underearning: You can see clearly how pervasive it has become in your life. This list should be a source of self-esteem for you. It was an act of courage to make it.

To remind you that you're not alone and that many others have already broken the trail before you, here's what my own list looked like, from the years just before I stopped debting:

- Visa
- MasterCard
- American Express
- Sears
- Macy's
- Kingston Oil Company
- Rondout National Bank
- Chemical Bank
- New York Telephone Company
- The Authors Guild
- Con Edison
- PEN American Center
- The Carnegie Fund
- Book packager
- Auto mechanic
- Dentist
- Landlord
- Parents
- Attorney

- Two literary agents
- Three friends

Underearners are very good at finding enablers.

9. Underearners Have Only a Vague Idea of What Their Expenses Are.

Beyond the rent and a close guess on utilities, most under-earners cannot tell you how much they spend each month, or on what.* An exaggeration?

How much did *you* spend last month?

How much did you spend on clothes? On newspapers, magazines? In coffee shops and on fast food? On cabs? On entertainment? On cosmetics? Laundry?

Harold, a carpenter, after keeping a record of every expenditure he made for two months, discovered that he was spending nearly a thousand dollars a year on coffee to go from delicatessens and diners. One thousand after-tax dollars—that's a big chunk of money to be ignorant about.

For most underearners, the money comes in, the money goes out—who knows where?—and there's never quite enough. This financial fog, this cloud of unknowing, is part of the general malaise that underearners experience over their money. You remain ignorant about your money, in the dark, blind, and helpless.

10. Underearners Are Workaholic, or Work in Cycles of Excess and Collapse, or Don't Want to Work at All.

You put in long hours at your job or profession; you work late into the night and on weekends. You often feel that you're

---

* This isn't true of underearners in debt recovery, who usually can.

behind schedule, or have a sense of urgency, feel that you can meet a deadline only with extra effort, that little stands between you and disaster but your own willingness to keep going.

Or you drive yourself mercilessly only so long as seems necessary, or while your enthusiasm is high, and then at the end collapse and are barely able to perform the minimum expected or required of you. During this latter time you feel blunted, sleep a lot, and have little will for anything, not even recreation. But sooner or later, because you have to or because you've managed to recharge yourself, you pick up the pace again and enter once more into the workaholic phase of the cycle. Underearners who work in this cyclical fashion are often self-employed.

(This is not the rhythm followed by athletes, performers, or others whose occupations lend themselves to working in intense bursts followed by periods of rest. In those cases the work periods are generally shorter and the fallow periods intentional, not the result of exhaustion or will-lessness.)

Steve, for example, who sells financial instruments, will work ten and twelve hours a day, go into his office on Saturdays, and bring work home until he makes a couple of large sales, earning big commissions. Then for weeks, sometimes months, he'll put in no more than an hour or two a day—the minimum he needs to keep his business going—and spend most of his time sleeping, puttering, sitting in front of his computer browsing aimlessly through information services, and going to movies.

Or you may not want to work at all. You might be fully conscious of this and resent and actively resist working at anything that requires much effort of you or that doesn't please you completely. More commonly, you'll simply move from job to job, never satisfied, always finding fault. Or you'll manage to get yourself fired and spend long periods unem-

ployed, convincing yourself and others that you really are looking for a job. Or you conceive of yourself as suffering from
some debility that prevents you from working more than part
time or at all.

Teri, a window designer who came from a well-to-do family in Chicago, had never supported herself more than mini-
mally. She married a musician who was also an underearner.
Every few months her family sent them a sizable check to help
them out. When Teri's marriage went bad and she got divorced, she was so upset she couldn't work. Her family supported her for a year while she went to therapy and studied
yoga. When she did return to work, her income was about
half of what her basic expenses were, with the slack again
taken up by her family. Two years later, her ex-husband fell ill.
Teri stopped working in order to nurse him full time. Her
family supported them. Her ex-husband died six months later.
In mourning, Teri once more felt incapable of doing any work.
When, a year later, she finally did feel ready, she went back to
work not as a window designer—in a field where she was
experienced and, at least theoretically, might have been able to
earn good money—but as a yoga instructor and leader of
small workshops focused on grief and overcoming grief.
Sometimes she didn't earn enough in a month to cover her
rent.

In some form or another, your relationship to work is
distorted.

11. Underearners See the Gross, Not the Net.

You see the total figure, which is not the *real* figure. The real
figure is what you actually get in hand, to keep, after taxes. If
you are offered a job, for example, paying $52,000 a year, that
means to you that you will be paid $1,000 a week. You won't.
Depending on where you live—which dictates local taxes—
and the nature of nontax deductions, such as union dues and

copayment of health benefits, you could well end up being paid—truly paid—only $500 a week.

But you make your decision based on what seems to you to be twice that much.

In practical terms, the gross is a fantasy. The discrepancy between the gross and the net can be enormous. In New York City, for example, a self-employed plumber reporting his thirtieth $1,000 of taxable income is going to pay about $610 of that in various taxes and levies. So he is not making $1,000 on a job he contracts for $1,000—he is making *$390*.

Sometimes this failure to see the net can be more subtle. A few years ago, I was involved in difficult negotiations over the advance for a book I was going to write. I knew how long it would take me and precisely what my true bottom line was—how much I needed in order not to run out of money and risk debt before I could finish the book. Finally, the publisher met that figure—just barely—and we closed the deal. Only a week later did I discover that the publisher had been negotiating on the basis of a three-part payment to be made over eighteen months, while *I* had made *my* calculations based on a two-part payment to be made over twelve months. In this case, the gross (the total of the advance) was still the same, but the effective net (the portion I would receive in one year) was only two-thirds of that. By not being clear about the terms and conditions of the deal, I had, in effect, seen the gross instead of the net.

12. Underearners May Think There Is Spiritual or Political Virtue in Not Having Money.

In a recent issue of a professional journal, a correspondent wrote (approvingly): "the *real* radicals are those doing the micropresses. They are radical by virtue of their intentional under-involvement in the mainstream economy."

This illustrates a particularly clever feat of magic some

underearners perform—they convince themselves that the result of their underearning, their lack of money, is actually a choice they made, and one that is moreover politically or spiritually virtuous.

When it's political virtue that is perceived, there is likely also to be resentment of those who do have money. There may be an adversarial view of life, too: us against them, management versus labor, exploiters over the downtrodden. To be sure, injustices do exist, and many people hold political positions and support economic theories of this nature who are not underearners. But if, along with this vision, you have a number of the other identifying characteristics as well, then your view is probably mostly a justification of—and function of—your underearning.

Chris, for example, arrived in New York at the height of the dope-smoking, antiwar, smash-the-establishment 1970s, found a home in an urban commune, and went to work for a socialist publication. For ten years he lived on very little money and a lot of ideology. Finally, tiring of that and somewhat disillusioned, he got a job with a corporation as a semi-skilled worker. Shortly, he became involved in union militancy. Chris now manages to pay his bills, but just barely, and he fills most of his nights with social-volunteer work and evening classes at a university, where he is taking a graduate degree in public health. As a gesture of solidarity with his fellow workers, whom he believes are being exploited by the company for which he works, he has twice refused promotions. Meanwhile, he continues to underearn.

More poignant is the underearner who believes there is spiritual value in being poor. Most of these people have a close relationship with a particular religion or a history of spiritual searching. They don't normally resent others who have money, but sometimes they do feel a flare of envy or wish wistfully that somehow they could have just a bit more. They may believe it is God's will for them not to, or even that they are being punished, and rightly, for some past transgression or fundamental defect. Or they may think they need to pray more for acceptance, to learn how to be joyful in the face of lack.

Many venerable spiritual traditions—at least in some of their teachings—suggest that eschewing money, possessions, and other things of this world can be beneficial and is perhaps even necessary to spiritual development. On the other hand, every tradition places great value on helping to eliminate poverty, or the ravages of poverty, from the world—which would hardly be the case if poverty were in itself ennobling or beneficial. What most people forget about Saint Francis, for example, is that he was an extremely wealthy young man who renounced his family's fortune, who *chose* to live a mendicant's life, who exercised an *option*. As was, and did, Gautama Buddha. There is a world—perhaps even a universe—of difference between voluntary renunciation and underearning.

13. Underearners Are Proud of Their Ability to Make Do with Little.

You pride yourself on being tough, a survivor. You don't need much—you can make do, get by. You see yourself as lean, mean, and smart. You know where to buy at discount, how to shop for bargains. Maybe you're working off the books and think you're beating the system, that you're a rogue, an adventurer, an existential hero. Or maybe you don't feel that way at all, but simply under siege, pressed hard just to make it through another day, deprived, yearning to have more. Even in this case, though, you're still likely to be proud of your ability to get by with so little.

Ted, a bike messenger, saw himself as a kind of urban pirate, a bicycling freebooter zipping in and out of clogged traffic, running lights, beating cabs to turns. He worked for cash, hit and ran. Most people knew him only by his first name. He lived in a rent-controlled apartment that had been passed from hand to hand for money to people like himself. Occasionally his bravado would fail. Then he would be either swept up in anger or thrown into despair over the meagerness of his life. But always he would return to his rogue's pose and boast again of his freedom from the system.

Susan, a bookkeeper who had worked for the same company for a decade, and had never asked for a raise or been offered one, lived in a fifth-floor walkup that she furnished largely with cast-off articles she found on the street. Though embarrassed by her circumstances, she held her carriage erect, moved with cultured grace, in the manner of disenfranchised royalty, and spoke with obvious pride of her resourcefulness and ability to satisfy all her needs.

14. Underearners Believe *Their* Occupation Won't Allow Them to Make More Money.

You're a painter, writer, or flautist—and everyone knows they can't make any money. Or you're a librarian, chimney sweep, university professor, butcher, baker, or candlestick maker. And everyone knows they can't make any money either. Or maybe you work on the packing line at the local cannery, and it's the only game in town.

Whatever it is you do, you're convinced not only that it pays very little—just enough to make ends meet, with a bit left over for a movie or two—but that it always will. And in fact it may *not* be a very high-paying occupation. But that doesn't mean there aren't ways you can glean additional income from it, or other, much-higher-paying activities you could do in addition to it. It's also possible that you selected this occupation—if there is truly little chance of your making more than a subsistence living at it—on an unconscious level, as part of your underearning. Or that you remain in your one-shop town or can't find anything higher-paying to do in addition to your job for the same reason.

Some underearners work in jobs or professions that pay well or even very well. In these cases, they generally manage like Valerie, the performance artist, to set conditions up so that their expenses devour most of their income. Or like John, a lawyer, they force themselves out of that occupation. John, who had his law degree from Yale, managed over the course of a half-dozen years to offend and alienate nearly everyone he worked with, one by one, until with a final, flamboyant gesture, he burned his last bridge behind him and left the practice of law altogether. After drifting through various jobs, he ended up tutoring graduate students in English.

Other underearners who work in high-paying occupations or professions keep themselves in the lowest income tiers of their field, go into civil service where they make less than they would in the private sector, work for low pay for nonprofit organizations, or comport themselves in such a fashion that they are among the first to be laid off in an economic downswing, the last to be rehired elsewhere.

15. Underearners Often Have Clothes and Other Possessions That Are Old, Worn Out, or Insufficient.

Much of what fills your life—clothes, kitchen equipment, furniture—is old, worn out, flawed, or second-rate. You may not even be aware of this, have only a vague sense of tawdriness or insufficiency. If you *are* aware of it, you probably think there's nothing you can do about it at the moment, or you tell yourself that these possessions are still serviceable, that you can get by with them.

Your closets are filled with clothes that are years out of

style or that haven't fit in memory. You hang on to old appliances—a clock-radio whose alarm no longer works, a toaster that toasts in only one slot or whose sides heat up, burning your fingers. You have frayed towels, or you sleep on a mattress that's past its day and is now uncomfortable. When Elizabeth, a secretary, began to free herself from underearning, she found an accumulation of clothes in her apartment that dated back nearly fifteen years, to her high school years.

Conversely, you might be very aware of your possessions and weed out and discard the unsuitable as soon as it becomes so, keeping only what's good. In this case, you probably own only the minimum required. Mark, a physical trainer, had one pair of excellent dress shoes, two fine dress shirts, and three ties. These, along with a good blazer and a pair of dress pants, made up his entire formal wardrobe. For casual wear, he had only a bit more. He had enough underwear to last a week and a single set of sheets and pillowcases. Everything else he owned, from his television set to an area rug, was of good quality, but he had only just enough to get by on. Whenever something wore out or began to malfunction and he had to replace it, he became fretful and upset.

16. Underearners Feel That Eventually *Something* Will Happen to Make Things Better.

You have a vague feeling that sooner or later, somehow, in some way, something will happen that will make your life better. Occasionally that feeling might be loosely attached to the thought: "Well, the economy will pick up. Then things will be easier."

At the height of this last recession, Julie, an artist and occasional university teacher, was speaking of the difficulties she was experiencing because of it: Buyers had become more cautious, schools had cut back on programs. "These are hard times," she said. She was behind in her rent, had little money beyond what she needed for food and clothing for herself and her six-year-old son. Indeed the economy had changed, and things were more difficult than they had been. But what Julie didn't recognize—and what shocked her when it was pointed out to her—was that her income now was only slightly less than it had been during the booming 1980s. Back then, her life had been just as much of a struggle for her as it was now. It wasn't the economy that was responsible for her lack and deprivation; it was her own underearning.

Sometimes an underearner is waiting for, wishing for, or planning on the Big Fix. The Big Fix will enable him to pay off all his debts and have a lot left over, or at the very least bring in enough to handle everything on a monthly basis, and life will become easier and looser. If this is you, you're going to:

- Get a raise
- Make a big sale
- Receive a gift from your grandmother
- Pick up the annual bonus
- Make a killing in the market
- Sell your stamp collection
- Receive an inheritance
- Graduate and go to work
- Sell the movie rights
- Win an insurance case
- Bring in an oil well

The Big Fix rarely arrives. If it does, it doesn't fix anything at all. The money is either already owed or somehow disappears in a year or two, and sooner or later you end up in the same place again.

In my own case, I'd been living with my wife and children

on $30,000 a year. It was the mid-1970s. One of my novels broke out, was optioned for film, selected by several book clubs, and sold very well. That summer I received a royalty check for $50,000. By the time I paid off all the significant debts, celebrated a bit, and undertook some renovations on the house, there wasn't much left. A year later, life was pretty much what it had been before. I was back in the cycle of borrowing and paying off, running out of money, borrowing and paying off, and running out of money again.

17. Underearners Fill Their "Free" Time with Endless Little Tasks and Chores.

You have little time for play. You always have more to do than time in which to do it. You often feel you're falling behind, or guilty that you don't accomplish enough. The house is never really clean, the bills haven't been cleared, there is filing to do, phone calls to return, dry cleaning to drop off. Your closet needs organizing, you haven't spent enough time with the kids, the car should be brought in for an oil change, and the floor ought to be washed.

Behind this near ceaseless doing, generally, lies the fear that you're running out of money, that there won't be enough. It's as if you think that somehow, if you keep busy, keep *accomplishing*, then catastrophe will be averted and you can make it through one more day, one more week.

Edgar is a hotel reservation clerk. He has difficulty sustaining relationships with women. Eventually his lack of money makes him feel either worthless or resentful that the woman he's seeing has more than he does. In addition to working at his job, Edgar cleans his apartment thoroughly each month, takes classes two nights a week, often feeling pressured by the need to study for exams or write papers, teaches remedial reading as a volunteer, and spends nearly as much time entering information about his extensive library of music into his computer as he does listening to the music.

Joyce, a nurse in Philadelphia, irons all of her three children's clothes, including their blue jeans and T-shirts, constantly makes small repairs and improvements in the house, teaches Sunday school, and is never comfortable sitting down to read or watch television.

A few underearners are just the opposite: They often feel lethargic or listless, putter halfheartedly, sleep long hours, and watch a lot of television. But most need to keep accomplishing.

18. Underearners Fear Spending Money and Feel Resentful When They Must—But Sometimes Go on Buying Binges.

You put off making large purchases—a CD player, a television set, a suit—or even smaller purchases, like towels. You're intimidated by the cost, grow anxious when you think about buying the item. You're afraid of making a mistake, of getting the wrong model or discovering later that you could have found it at a better price somewhere else. Sometimes, when you do have some money, this fear shows up as hesitation or indecisiveness: Do you *really* want to go to the mountains for a week? Or: Yes, there seems to be enough now, but what about the fall, when the kids will need new clothes for school? Maybe you shouldn't go, maybe you should keep this money in reserve.

When you *must* spend, it's painful to watch your balance drop—as you write out checks for the rent, car insurance, phone bill. Even taking money out of your wallet to pay for food, diminishing the number of bills you have, may upset you.

But for all this fear of spending money and the resentment

you may feel when you must, you sometimes go on a buying binge. Suddenly, on what seems nearly an irresistible impulse, you'll leave your home on a Saturday morning, hurry to Macy's or Neiman Marcus, and buy a winter coat—one more costly than you've been planning on—and then, telling yourself you deserve them, that you need them, you'll go on to buy a scarf, leather gloves, a couple of sweaters, and boots.

A buying binge doesn't have to involve a lot of money; sometimes less than a hundred dollars, sometimes less than fifty. In that case, it will probably involve several small items, and you will do it with a sense of giddiness or euphoria, or soaring feelings of pride or self-love.

Often a buying binge is followed by an emotional crash, with feelings of guilt and self-recrimination, even self-hatred. You might return some of the items; if you do, handing them back to the clerk will probably depress you, make you feel somehow stolen from.

19. Underearners Believe Money Would Cure All Their Problems.

You may not consciously think that money would make you taller, prettier, better able to relate to members of the opposite sex, more talented, happier in your work, or a scholar, an officer, and a gentleman, but deep within you, at some level, you *do* believe it. You believe money would do all this for you, and more. Chronic underearners, at some level or another, believe money would cure all their problems.

Money won't. It can't. In fact, money can't even cure underearning.

But recovery from underearning can and *will* bring about a massive healing within you, which will eliminate a fundamental source of pain and deprivation. In turn, this healing will generate positive reverberations across the spectrum of your life, enabling you to deal more effectively with whatever other problems and concerns you may have.

Did you see yourself reflected in this chapter? If you did, it's not surprising. I found myself here. So did every one of the many other underearners I've spoken with over the past several years. And I'd lay odds that every one of the millions more who are suffering from underearning across the country at this moment would see themselves here, too. If they didn't, I'd be astonished—and skeptical.

Remember: Having a few of these characteristics (a list will be given at the end of the chapter) does not make you, or anyone else, an underearner. Nearly everyone will exhibit some of them. It's even possible to demonstrate several and still not be an underearner. But if you have most of them, or even a majority, then you probably are an underearner, and—at the very least—could benefit by taking steps to correct that. In the end, underearning is a self-diagnosed condition.

The first clear look at yourself in relationship to underearning, if you are or think you might be an underearner, can be a shock. But actually, seeing yourself here is the best thing that could have happened. It's a quantum leap in awareness of why you have been living in pain and lack, and without such awareness there can be no change.

Regardless of how long you have been underearning or how powerfully the malady has gripped you, you can, if you work this program, free yourself from underearning forever— even if that underearning has been compulsive. Emancipation won't take place overnight. It's a process. Some people require longer than others. But it *can* and *will* take place.

So what happens in the meantime? Are you condemned to keep on underearning until you are deep into the process?

No.

By beginning to use the concepts, principles, and techniques that follow, which together constitute Prospering, *you can bring your underearning to a halt right now.* You can reverse your situation and begin to liberate yourself *immediately*—despite the lingering presence of any dysfunctional attitudes and beliefs you might have about yourself, money, or yourself in relationship to money, despite the number of years you have been underearning, and despite your fears to the contrary.

All you have to do is turn to the next chapter.

Here, for review, is a list of the characteristics discussed in this chapter:

Underearners

1. Underearners are usually in debt.
2. Underearners have little savings, few assets.
3. Underearners are often in financial crisis.
4. Underearners feel pain, stress, and fear over money.
5. Underearners do a lot of unpaid work: volunteer, charity, or showcase work.
6. Underearners often come from alcoholic or otherwise troubled families.
7. Underearners may resent people with money.
8. Underearners are good at finding enablers.
9. Underearners have only a vague idea of what their expenses are.
10. Underearners are workaholic, or work in cycles of excess and collapse, or don't want to work at all.
11. Underearners see the gross, not the net.
12. Underearners may think there is spiritual or political virtue in not having money.

13. Underearners are proud of their ability to make do with little.

14. Underearners believe *their* occupation won't allow them to make more money.

15. Underearners often have clothes and other possessions that are old, worn out, or insufficient.

16. Underearners feel that eventually *something* will happen to make things better.

17. Underearners fill their "free" time with endless little tasks and chores.

18. Underearners fear spending money and feel resentful when they must—but sometimes go on buying binges.

19. Underearners believe money would cure all their problems.

PART II
FUNDAMENTALS

3.

GETTING UNDER WAY

THIS AND THE REMAINING PARTS OF THE BOOK CONTAIN THE working elements of Prospering—a basic program of liberation from underearning.

Prospering is a complete program. It contains every concept and technique you need in order to free yourself from underearning. But it does not and cannot include all the many other practices, disciplines, and insights that can enhance and expand that freedom. You will, in your new awareness, encounter other practices that prove helpful. Do not hesitate to incorporate them into this program, building a structure of your own design.

WHAT DOES FREEDOM FROM UNDEREARNING *MEAN*?

Before we can even hope to free ourselves from underearning, we need a clear idea of what that condition might be. Basic freedom (or recovery) for an alcoholic means that one day at a time he or she does not have to drink. Basic freedom for an underearner means that one day at a time he or she does not have to underearn. In its essential form, then:

Freedom from underearning means regularly to gain income that is enough to meet your needs in a humane way.

It also means—thereby—to be delivered from the pain and negative practical consequences of underearning.

It does *not* mean that you will *necessarily* bring in large amounts of money. You may, you may not. That there will be *an* increase is certain, and that freedom from underearning is possible for anyone who works this program is unconditional.

There are further levels of liberation—or perhaps more accurately, *dimensions* of it—available to those who choose to pursue them. Most of these are internal, but they do affect external conditions. Some people think of them as a spiritual voyage; others as simply creating a better, more satisfying life.

How far one wishes to travel on this road is always a personal choice.

Let's turn now to Prospering's techniques.

HERE THE PRACTICAL, THERE THE SPIRITUAL

This and the next three chapters contain practical techniques. The techniques in later chapters are just as effective, perhaps even more so, but they are primarily spiritual—or, if you prefer, psychological. Both are important. The practical have immediate positive impact, while the spiritual bring about the kind of fundamental internal changes that are necessary if your liberation from underearning is to become permanent.

Now and then, the practical and the spiritual may be the same. (In a larger sense the spiritual is always practical, but that's beyond the scope of this book to discuss.) Yoga, for example, can be looked upon both as a physical exercise and a spiritual practice. Yet a given individual may undertake it primarily or even solely for one or the other. Do not allow yourself to become bothered by my having placed a particular concept, technique, or action into one category rather than another; just reposition it wherever you wish.

Don't Shoot, I Surrender

It is absolutely necessary to accept that you are an underearner.

This is a hard thing for most people to do. But without such acceptance, you'll only be applying Band-Aids. There will be no real change. If you have doubts about the reason you lack sufficient money in your life, or if you feel angry, panicky, or in despair over the possibility that you might be an underearner, set those doubts and emotions aside as best you can for the moment.

And alone, in a quiet private place, as best you can, surrender: Admit to yourself that you have a problem with underearning, and that it has caused a lot of pain and trouble in your life.

Do it now.

Good. Take a breath and relax. Now try it again. Let it settle in. Let yourself feel the truth of it: You have a problem with underearning. It has caused a lot of pain and trouble in your life.

Many people experience a sense of relief when they finally admit this to themselves. Their response is: "Thank God! Now I know what the problem is. Which means that I can fix it." Others react quite differently. They panic and bolt for the door, or want to punch out whoever made the suggestion.

Resistance to surrender, which stems from fear, is based largely on a misconception of what the word means. If you're like most people, you interpret surrender as meaning a loss of freedom, defeat, weakness. But one of its primary definitions is:

To give something up in favor of something else.

It is simply letting go an old way of doing things in order to embrace a new way. When you admit that you have a problem with underearning, when you surrender to that, you become willing to let go of your old perceptions and behaviors, which resulted in deprivation, pressure, and unhappiness, and in their place to embrace new ones, which bring about freedom, ease, and thriving. This surrender, paradoxically, is your first triumph.

If you cannot truly surrender at this point, if deep within you rebel against the possibility that you are an underearner, then *act as if.* Just for now, act *as if* you were an underearner: Follow the program of liberation outlined here. If eventually you think it is inappropriate for you, you can simply stop. You have nothing to lose and much to gain.

Defusing Denial

Denial is the refusal to admit that you have a problem. It's an attempt to rationalize or justify your underearning. Denial is a wholly natural reaction. It's also a dangerous one. If you buy it, you're not going to have much success in ever bringing in enough money to meet your needs in a humane way.

Denial is nearly universal at first—after all, no one *wants* to have an underearning problem. You tell yourself it's your parents' fault, the government's fault, your wife's fault. It's the economy's fault, the patriarchy's, the banks', the credit card companies', your boss's fault, society's fault. It's the divorce, you say to yourself, the job market, late-paying accounts, taxes, interest rates, the new roof, high rents. Anything or anyone but you, even though you're the one who repeatedly gains less income than you need or than would be beneficial.

Actually, your underearning isn't your fault, not in the sense that you're flawed or that you did something wrong and are guilty and deserve punishment. You didn't plan this, you didn't deliberately set out to put yourself in this position. Neither did I nor any of the other several millions of people who are standing right alongside you. There's no blame in this; it was not intentional. But denial is a serious problem nonetheless.

Sometimes denial can be subtle. Hilary, a writer, resisted the idea that she was an underearner for some time. When finally she allowed that she did have a bit of a problem here, she began to refer to herself as a *temporary* underearner—imminently to become an overearner. By using the word *temporary*, she continued to deny that she was by nature an underearner and suggested instead that this was only a passing condition, not typical of the normal state of her life. So Hilary continued (with brief interruptions) to underearn—until the point, tentatively, where she began to think and behave as if she might truly *be* an underearner, perhaps even a compulsive one. Then, steadily, her income began to rise.

Resistance to the idea of being an underearner, especially a chronic or compulsive underearner, is quite reasonable. It would seem, at first glance, that if I am a *compulsive* under-earner, then I am condemned to continue underearning—compulsively—for the rest of my life. But that is no more true than it is that to admit one is an alcoholic condemns one to go on drinking for the rest of one's life. Just the opposite. By admitting she is an alcoholic, a woman begins to free herself from her need to drink. By admitting he is an underearner, a man begins to free himself from his need to underearn. So long as they are in denial, she is condemned to keep drinking as she struggles to prove she is powerful over alcohol and not an alcoholic, and he is condemned to keep underearning as he struggles to prove he is powerful over earning and not an underearner. (We'll deal with this troublesome question of powerlessness, and what it means and doesn't mean, in Chapter 8.)

Sometimes, too, there is an element of superstitious think-ing in denial, a fear that to call oneself an underearner will be to create the reality, that to use a demon's name is to summon the demon up. Psychologically, there's a grain of truth in this. But the fact remains that if one *is* an underearner, then no amount of denying it is ever going to change that reality; in-deed, it will only worsen the condition.

Just for now, admit, if you can, that you have a problem of at least some kind with underearning. The turnaround begins with surrender—and denial can be as lethal to surrender as a bullet.

To combat denial:

1. Freely admit it's there. Tell yourself that of course you'd rather not be an underearner—who would? But recognize that personal preference doesn't change the facts. I'd much rather be six-foot-two and have a full head of hair again. But I'm not, and I don't. I have preferences, but they don't change the facts.

2. Reread Chapters 1 and 2. Remember that the material within them isn't theoretical; it's been drawn from the lives of countless people who are in serious trouble with underearning. Write down the number of times you find yourself there, to impress that fact upon yourself.

3. Remember that you're not unique. Having this problem doesn't place you in a tiny minority who somehow haven't been able to make things work; there are literally millions of Americans in precisely the same situation.

4. Drive home to yourself that surrender doesn't sentence you to a life of poverty and difficulty. Just the opposite—it's your first step on the road to freedom from that.

5. Proceed as if you didn't have any denial. Don't let it sidetrack you from your purpose. Denial is simply that, denial. It can't force you to do anything. You can go right ahead with this program despite its presence. In time, with repeated constructive action, its grip will lessen.

Sometimes denial goes dormant a while, only to pop up again later. It often reappears after you've begun to reverse your situation and the stress is easing—or with a large influx of money, from whatever source. The old attitudes and behavior patterns don't die easily. They may simply have gone into hiding, biding their time, only to break into the open again at the first good opportunity.

Everyone has such moments. My own internal dialogue usually goes something like this: "You know, I really appreciate all the help and good wishes, and indeed it was quite useful, but I think there's been a misunderstanding here. You see, I was simply depressed after my divorce, it was a slow time in my career, I had some large responsibilities, and I made a couple of mistakes. That's really all there was to it. I'm fine now, so thanks a lot and all the best to you. I'll be moving on now."

This kind of thinking is a one-way ticket right back to the place you started from. If denial does resurface later, and you're tempted to say, "Thanks, and so long," return to this section and go through the defusing procedures once more.

THINGS *NOT* TO DO

One definition of insanity is to keep doing the same thing over and over again and expect different results. It is helpful, therefore, to establish a threshold of behavior to avoid, one day at a time, if you want to become free of underearning.

With alcohol, if one avoids picking up the first drink one day at a time, one can't possibly get drunk. With underearning, if one avoids certain conduct one day at a time, it is difficult, if not impossible, to continue underearning. There are also actions to *take* that are beneficial, but those will be presented in the following chapters. Here we are concerned with what *not* to do.

Do Not Debt

It is necessary, as an initial step, for you to stop the overt behavior connected with underearning. Only then will it be possible for you to work effectively on the elements that underlie it, such as dysfunctional perceptions of money and self. Unless you stop the behavior first, liberation is not possible.

Again, the analogy with alcoholism is useful. An alcoholic

may go to therapy, attend meetings of a support group, exercise, practice excellent nutrition, try to work the Twelve Steps, and undertake any number of other laudable activities, but if he continues to drink, then everything else he does will be useless—there will be no liberation. Once he *stops* drinking, however, one day at a time, then everything else he does in the service of his liberation will be of benefit to him. So also with underearners and debting.

Debt is a form of poverty—and one of the cruelest. It gives you the *illusion* of having more money than you do. When you use credit cards, department-store charge accounts, or overdraft checking privileges; when you let a bill go unpaid, or take a salary advance or loan from an institution or a friend; then you *think* you have more money than you do, you *think* you're bringing in more of it than you actually are. Unsecured credit—debt—is the most common and frequently turned-to enabler that underearners have. Borrowing money or using credit only helps an underearner delude herself, only staves off the consequences, the inevitable bottoming-out, awhile longer.

How, if you continue to borrow money to meet your basic expenses, do you expect that you will ever stop underearning?

The very act of borrowing, of using credit, of not paying a bill on time, is a clear signal that you are gaining less income than you need. And so long as you consider the use of some form of debt to be a valid option for meeting your needs, then it is nearly impossible that you will become free of underearning.

Not-debting is a large subject in itself. The most important point to make about it here is that if your commitment not to debt, one day at a time, is unconditional, then you will *always* find ways to succeed at it, to cut expenses, or more important, to bring in more money—and that is the beginning of liberation from underearning.

The commitment is what empowers.

Not all underearners are debtors. Most, but not all. So what about those who aren't? Is it necessary for them too to avoid using a credit card when they go out to dinner, or charging a television at a department store? If you are such a person, if you pay your credit card balance in full each month, if you're never late with your rent or mortgage payment, if you hardly ever dip into your checking overdraft privilege, and have rarely borrowed unsecured money, then—while still advisable and desirable—it is probably not absolutely *necessary* for you to forgo using unsecured credit. But don't delude yourself here. If you have or have ever had any trouble at all with debt or unpaid bills, then you need, one day at a time, not to incur any new debt. This is the largest single contribution you can make toward your liberation.

You'll find that not incurring new debt is easier to do than you thought, as you work the other parts of Prospering. Reciprocally, not-debting will in turn help you to work those other parts more easily. As relentless as was our decline while we were underearning, so, in the reverse, is our liberation: Freedom from underearning is progressive.

For one day, just for today, *do not debt.*

Do Not Take Work That Pays You Less Than You Need

This would seem obvious, but for underearners, it isn't—an underearner nearly *always* takes work that pays him less than he needs.

Underearners do not see that the employment they obtain, the assignments they accept, the contracts they sign, and the projects they undertake nearly always bring them less income than they need to meet their basic expenses, or just barely enough with a little left over. Underearners do not relate the money they accept to the amount they have to spend in order to live.

This blindness occurs for several reasons. They may be in a financial crisis and need money immediately; they may fear that if they don't take this job or deal, there won't be anything else; they may not know what their expenses are; they may see the gross, not the net; and others.

Two approaches will help you circumvent this.

First: Become clear about your expenses.

Second: Maintain awareness that it is your reflex to take less money than you need.

Expenses

The easiest way to become clear about your expenses is to keep a record of them on a daily basis for at least two months. This requires some effort, but isn't near as bothersome or time-consuming as you might fear.

A Spending Record can be a powerful tool and a key factor in liberating yourself from underearning. It is so helpful, in fact, that most people who get free of underearning decide to keep one on an ongoing basis. The Spending Record is *not* a budget. It is simply a record of the money you actually *do* spend. It allows you to see—possibly for the first time— how much you spend, and precisely where your money is going.

All you need to do is jot down the amount, when you make a cash expenditure, and note what it was for. Some people keep a little spiral notebook in their purse or briefcase. I carry a pen and a folded piece of paper in my wallet. When you pay for something by check, be sure to record in your checkbook what that check was for, such as household furnishings, clothes, or recreational equipment. A check written out to Macy's, for example, with no other indication, doesn't tell you what the money was spent on.

At the end of each week, total up your expenses.

Here's a simplified example of what a one-week Spending Record might look like:

July 1–7	
Rent	$860.00
Groceries	78.54
Clothes	19.50
Entertainment	19.00
Laundry	11.25
Medical	4.89
Telephone	47.18
Transportation	12.50
Total:	$1,052.86

Most people break their spending into twenty-five to thirty-five categories. Avoid extremes at either end. Too few, and you're still enveloped in fog. Too many, and you overcomplicate the record.

The only hard and fast rule with the Spending Record is to be precise. If you have an especially heavy expense, such as therapy, it's best to make that a separate category rather than to subsume it in your Medical category. If you're a passionate skier and spend a lot on equipment, clothes, lessons, travel, and resorts, it's best to make Skiing a separate category. If you were to put those expenses variously under, say, Clothes, Recreation, and Travel, you wouldn't really know how much you actually spend on this activity.

The following is a list of the most common categories.

Some won't apply to you, and you'll probably need a few that don't appear here:

- Alimony
- Books
- Cabs/limousines
- Car (gasoline, tires, maintenance, insurance, repair)
- Children's expenses (see Chapter 6)
- Child support
- Clothes
- Cosmetics
- Dry cleaning
- Education
- Food out (fast food, diners)
- Gas/electricity
- Gifts
- Groceries
- Haircuts/beauty salon
- Hobby
- Home equipment (television, radio, dishes, pots and pans, appliances, tools)
- Home furnishings (tables, chairs, beds, rugs, drapes)
- Home heating
- Home repair/maintenance (painting, plumbing, wiring, storm windows, heating system, roofing, insurance, landscaping)
- Home supplies (paper towels, sponges, dish and laundry soap, steel-wool pads, toilet paper, scouring powder, floor wax, string, tape)
- House cleaning
- Income taxes (if assessed beyond amount withheld)
- Investments

- Laundry
- Life insurance
- Magazines/newspapers
- Medical (doctors, prescriptions, glasses)
- Medical insurance
- Personal care (shampoo, nail scissors, soap, razors and blades, toothbrushes, hairbrushes, combs, perfume or cologne)
- Personal growth (lectures, seminars, special training or courses)
- Pet
- Professional dues
- Property taxes
- Rent/mortgage
- Sport
- Telephone
- Therapy
- Tuition
- Vacation/travel
- Vitamins
- Miscellaneous (any little oddity that doesn't fit into the other categories; however, if the total here is consistently over $20, you probably need a new category or two)

To make a monthly Spending Record, divide the month into four one-week periods (with the final "week," of course, being seven to ten days long). At the end of the month, add the weekly expenses in each category to arrive at the month's total for that category. Then add the totals of the categories to arrive at a grand total. This tells you exactly how much you spent that month, and on what. Many people incorporate their weekly records into their monthly record, combining them to make one form.

A simplified monthly record might look like this:

SPENDING RECORD FOR JULY					
Week	1	2	3	4	Total
Rent	860.00				860.00
Food	78.54	83.20	76.15	94.89	332.78
Clothes	19.50		7.67	31.23	58.40
Entertainment	14.00		17.50	6.00	37.50
Gas & Electricity		61.15			61.15
Laundry	11.25		16.75	5.80	33.80
Medical	4.89	65.00			69.89
Papers & Magazines	7.00	6.25	8.50	3.95	25.70
Telephone	47.18				47.18
Transportation	12.50	2.50	15.75	22.00	52.75
Totals:	1,054.86	218.10	142.32	163.87	1,579.15

The Spending Record will tell you a lot about how you live. My own first record—which I drew up ten years ago, in early debt recovery—didn't even contain an entertainment category. Ed, a tall soft-spoken southerner who works in advertising, pointed out its absence to me.

"The first thing you have to do," he said, "is to start spending money on yourself."

That statement was nearly incomprehensible to me then.

Nor did I have a category for personal care—toothpaste, antiperspirants, shoe polish, and such. I'd lumped those under Food, since that included everything I bought at the supermarket.

"And not just haircuts and toothpaste," Ed said, "but stuff like massages, though some people prefer to put that under the Health category. I think of it as Personal Care, myself."

"Massages?"

"Or yoga classes," he said. "Scuba diving, whatever. It's up to you. But one thing's certain—if you don't learn how to give to yourself and start enjoying life again, you're never going to get out of this."

The Spending Record can tell you a lot.

Creating one is a process. You'll alter it as your awareness grows and as change occurs in your life. I'm now on the seventh version of my own.

But while the Spending Record is revealing, and indeed a powerful tool, it cannot in itself reverse underearning. Many solvent debtors who carefully kept a Spending Record for years continued to underearn, managing to bring in only a little more than they needed to avoid new debt. If they did happen to make a large amount on occasion (particularly those who were self-employed or who worked on commission) then —as I and others did—they would resume their underearning shortly thereafter, in time exhaust their reserves, and end up hovering once again at the edge of debt. Since these were people who had little or no inkling that they were underearners, it's logical that the Spending Record, while it helped them stay out of debt, did little to help them get free of underearning. Once they recognized themselves as underearners, that changed.

Awareness

Reflexively, routinely, underearners take work that won't pay them enough to meet their basic needs or will pay just that and only a bit more. To prevent this lethal reflex, it's necessary to make awareness of it an integral part of your consciousness, so that it figures into every decision you make about whether to accept a job, project, or assignment. We're going to address that briefly here and discuss additional ways later.

In general, never accept or reject an offer at the moment it is made—no matter how powerful your emotional response or how strongly the offerer pressures you to do so. The exception might be an offer that comes after a period of negotiation, when you're clear on what your requirements are, or an offer involving so much or so little money that—taking a moment for reflection—you are certain whether it would be to your benefit or not. Otherwise, intervene in the process that makes you reflexively, routinely, take work that pays you less than you need. Say: "Thank you. That's an interesting offer. I'd like to think about it and get back to you. What would be the best time for me to call you tomorrow?"

Give yourself at least an hour to measure the offer against your needs (about which you have clear knowledge now, because of the Spending Record) and your disposition to underearn. If the money won't meet your needs—which include recreation, entertainment, and all the other categories that make life enjoyable, along with savings—then, with real thanks and appreciation (for it is never anyone's fault that what he wishes or can afford to pay you doesn't coincide with what you need to earn), decline the offer. To accept it would be consciously to underearn. (In Chapter 4 we'll discuss what to do if you're already working at a job that isn't paying you enough to meet your needs.)

There will be times when—because of fear that there's nothing else out there, or pressure from creditors, or the feeling that you must get at least *some* money in immediately, or other reasons—you'll feel that you have to accept an offer, even though it won't fully meet your needs.

Don't.

Do whatever you have to do in order not to debt—but otherwise, for one day, this day, turn it down.

For one day, this day, one day at a time: *Do not take work that pays you less than you need.*

Do Not Say No to Money

Underearners evade, avoid, and deflect money like running backs hurtling toward the goal line of poverty—touchdown!

Do not say no to money. Do not evade it, avoid it, or deflect it.

Let it into your life. We are talking, of course, about money that meets the first two criteria: money that isn't debt, and money that isn't less than you need. If it satisfies both of these, then do not say no to it.

Money is constantly in motion. Frequently, it comes looking for a way into *our* lives—more frequently than any underearner still in the grip of her affliction can possibly imagine. This is a consequence of its necessary, ceaseless activity. Money must keep moving. If it stops, it ceases to be money.

Even sitting "untouched" in a savings account, money is never really still—the bank lends it out, the borrower pays a contractor to build a house for him, the contractor buys materials from a supplier, the supplier pays his utility bill, the utility company uses it to pay its employees, its employees buy food, clothing. . . .

Money is never motionless. And in its movement, it approaches underearners as often as it does anyone else. But underearners evade it, avoid it, and deflect it.

Most of us short-circuit several potentially profitable notions every day. An idea pops into mind, we grow excited for an instant, and then we're overwhelmed by our negative chatter —"Oh, that would never work. . . . That's not me. . . .

I'd look like a fool. . . . It's hopeless. . . . I'm not qualified. . . . No one can make money that way." The idea
quickly slips away, we do nothing, and we continue to lan-
guish, yearning for a life we don't have and wishing things
were different.

We evade money by not following up. Sy, a psychotherapist, was astonished to watch himself fail to return a call to a
corporate vice-president who, after a series of meetings, left a
message on Sy's answering machine saying the company was
considering going to contract with him, would he please call
back as soon as he could. We avoid it by blinding ourselves to
opportunities. Erica is fast-witted and funny. She keeps her
friends in stitches. So's Mike. He keeps his friends in stitches
too. He also makes an extra $3,500 a year selling material
freelance to a publisher of joke greeting cards. We deflect it by
refusal: "I don't want to work for that company." "I'm not
ready to move yet." "I've never done anything like that."

Early in my own liberation from underearning, the com-
munications director of a large professional association called
me from Washington, D.C. She'd heard that I broke writer's
block for people. (I perked up, sensing income.) That was not
the problem *she* had. (I sagged.) Her staff writers were not
blocked. (I sagged further.) Their problem was burnout and
staleness, caused by having to write about the same topics over
and over. (Why was she calling me?) Could I help? (How?
What did I know about burnout in staff writers?) They could
pay $1,250 for an afternoon session with their four writers.

It was truly depressing to know that $1,250 was available,
but not for me.

I was about to express my regrets and thank her for the
call and tell her I hoped she could find an answer somewhere,
when—with the force of a hammer blow, nearly taking my
breath away, and causing the hand in which I held the phone
to begin sweating—I was struck by the realization that I had a

compulsion to underearn . . . and that I was about to turn down $1,250.

Perhaps, I thought, the reason I am about to turn this money down is not valid; perhaps it is a function of my compulsion to underearn. Though it was difficult, though my throat began to close and I had trouble getting the words out, I forced myself to say:

"Yes, I think I can help you with it. I'd like to give it some thought. Is there a time tomorrow afternoon that would be convenient for me to call you back?"

Six weeks later, I led a four-hour workshop for that woman and her writers down in Washington. I called it "Word Renewal." It was designed to rekindle creative vigor and enthusiasm among staff writers, eliminate staleness and burnout, and provide them with the concepts and techniques they needed never to fall victim to this kind of problem again. It was a great success.

Here was a case where money had actively sought me out —had even gone so far as to call me long distance. But still, because I am an underearner, I came within an exhalation of saying no to it.

One day at a time: *Do not say no to money.*

4.

RECONCEIVING

IN THE LAST CHAPTER WE CONCENTRATED ON THINGS *NOT* TO do to begin your liberation from underearning. Here and in the next two we're going to focus on things *to* do. The practical actions and techniques you'll use begin in Chapter 5. In this chapter, the techniques are largely conceptual—they address your *internal* world.

Much of your underearning has resulted from distorted attitudes and perceptions you have about money, about yourself, and about yourself in relationship to money. You need to be at least familiar with the techniques in this chapter, which are less tangible than later ones but equally important to Prospering, and the concepts behind them, before you can begin to take effective external action.

They begin with the more purely ideational and end with ones that involve some activity.

Read them carefully. Think about them. Work with them.

THINGS *TO* DO

Economies Are Personal

Realize that economies are personal.

You have your own individual economy, which is separate and apart from the national economy. In fact, so far as underearning is concerned, the larger economy is mostly irrelevant.

During most of the booming 1980s, when money was washing back and forth through the economy in great tidal waves and Americans were prospering as they rarely had before, I was making very little money—I and many other underearners. This was not because of any technological, social, or other kind of upheaval that had disoriented me or them. I could argue for that position (in my own case, the rise of video and cable TV, computers, changes in the publishing industry, a shrinking literacy rate), but that would be a specious argument, mostly a function of denial.

Weren't there *some* real reasons? Of course—but they came and went, and I was still underearning. And there were other people whose backgrounds and experiences were similar to mine—who got divorced, for example, or were writers—who *weren't* underearning. So something was different about me, something separated me from them. What that something was, was underearning.

Most recently, the recession of the early 1990s was (and to a degree remains) the great ogre: the bogeyman, scapegoat, and whipping boy of the moment, blamed by many for the fact that they are in debt or bringing in scarcely enough money to meet their needs. In some cases, that is true. But consider this: In the very midst of the booming 1980s, more than *20 million Americans*, from all classes, backgrounds, and walks of life, found themselves *overwhelmed* by personal debt. And this: Personal bankruptcy climbed by 300 percent during those prosperous years—to nearly 1 million people a year by the end of the decade.

On the other hand, at the height of the recession, and during the first full twelve-month period in which I practiced the principles and techniques of liberation from underearning, I brought in more money than I ever had in any other year of my life. In a year and a half of recuperating from underearning, Harriet, thirty-four, who was working as a table-photographer in a restaurant and barely getting by, became a professional illustrator and more than doubled her income. Alan, a machinist, moved to another company, while Sylvia, his wife, took a one-morning-per-week job at a sporting goods store (trading child-watching hours with a neighbor); together they raised their family income by twenty-five percent.

What these people and others with similar stories have in common is that each was an underearner who was earning scarcely enough to meet his or her needs in a prosperous economy*—and each of whom, once having undertaken a program of liberation, began to earn significantly more even though the economy was in a serious downturn.

There is no denying that the larger economy *does* have an impact. But the most it can generally dictate, barring complete collapse, is the *manner* in which you earn your living, not *whether* you can. An underearner will repeatedly gain less income than he or she needs even in the best of times. And an underearner in recovery will regularly gain at least enough to meet his or her needs, in a humane way, even in the worst of times. *Your* economy is personal.

---

* Prosperous in the sense that salaries were high, capital available, property values rising, and employment easy to come by. This was to a degree an illusion—the country itself was falling ever deeper into debt—but here we are dealing with *personal* recovery.

RIGHT NOW, YOU'RE PERFECTLY ALL RIGHT

Right now, at this very moment, you have:

1. A roof over your head
2. Clothes to wear
3. Food to eat

So right now, today, you are perfectly all right—you have everything you need, you don't lack for anything essential.

Simplistic? No. Simple? Yes.

Alex works in public relations. He was $40,000 in debt and financially paralyzed when he began to heal from under-earning. His emotions were chaotic, and his marriage was in trouble because of debt. Two and a half years later, he now meets all his monthly obligations without difficulty, and his lifestyle includes such restored amenities as vacations, theater, and dining out. He's much calmer, his marriage is strong again, and he has liquidated $19,000 of his debt. In his words, "This is a simple program for complicated people."

Right now, today, you are perfectly all right. You have everything you need. This is an anchor stone. Take a minute to do the following:

Close your eyes. Breathe deeply a couple of times. Relax your body and clear your mind. Ground yourself in this day, which is where you belong. It's not yesterday. It's not tomorrow. It is today. Picture the roof over your head. Today, at this moment, you are not living out in the elements. Visualize the clothes you're wearing. See the clothes that are in your closet, in your bureau drawer. Realize that today, right now, you do have clothes to wear. Now picture what you had for breakfast, what you had for lunch, for dinner. Connect with this. You have had, and you do have, all the food you need today.

Consider that, and know this to be absolutely true: Right

now, today, you have a place to live, clothes to wear, and food to eat.

Yesterday's gone, tomorrow isn't here yet. All that is real, ever, is today. And right now, today, you are perfectly all right. You have everything you need.

It's good to go through this process every morning. Shortly after you wake, before you get out of bed, sit for a minute or two, close your eyes, and visualize these things. It's a great way to start your day, knowing that you're perfectly all right and that you have everything you need.

At intervals throughout the day, take a few minutes to do the exercise again, especially if you begin to worry about or get depressed over bills and debts. Those emotions come because you're projecting into the future. You are responding to what you think is going to happen next week, next month, next year.

You don't know what's going to happen. Nobody does— nobody possibly can. So in truth, all you're reacting to is your own imagination (which bases *its* projections on the past, how you *used* to live). There is nothing real in that. Slow down when this occurs. Stop. Go off by yourself to a quiet place. Close your eyes and do this visualization exercise.

Reground yourself in today. Right now, today, is where you live. *And right now, today, you are perfectly all right.*

A THINKING PERSON'S THOUGHT

Would you be willing to stand up in front of a room full of strangers and tell them exactly how much you made last year and how much you owe? I ask that at the beginning of workshops I lead: How many people here would be willing to do that, right now? Hardly anyone ever raises a hand. Most begin to shift uncomfortably and avoid my eyes.

When I tell them I'm not going to ask anyone to do it, relief sweeps across the room.

Money is a highly charged subject. And most of the emotions people feel around it are negative: fear, shame, embarrassment, anger.

In those workshops, the bulk of the participants' negative emotions are centered on what the others might think of them. Next I tell them that I'm going to close my eyes for five or six seconds and remain silent. I do. When I open my eyes, most of them are looking at me expectantly. I ask if anyone experienced a significant change of mood while my eyes were closed. Now and then someone will say he became a little anxious, or felt pleasant, or relaxed, but mostly they look at me in puzzlement.

Then I tell them: "What I did while my eyes were closed was this. First, I thought the *worst* possible thought I could about all of you. Then I thought the *best* possible thought I could about all of you.

"Yet none of you was plunged into despair or got angry at me. Nor was anyone lifted into euphoria or overcome with affection toward me. The point is: What other people *think* about you cannot possibly *affect* you. *Their* thoughts cannot influence your mood. Only yours can—what *you* think."

And that is the truth. Test it for yourself. In a plane, restaurant, movie theater—anywhere—pick someone at random. For three seconds think the worst possible thought you can about her; then for three seconds think the best possible thought. Did she break down weeping? Did she burst into exaltation? Your thoughts cannot affect other people; nor can other people's thoughts affect you.

"Oh, yeah? Well, what about his thought, 'I'm going to fire your ass'?"

It can't affect you. Actions can, but thoughts can't.

Yet most underearners experience repeated negative emotions over what other people might think of them—friends, relatives, a spouse, children, store clerks, service personnel, bank tellers, shopkeepers, even someone on the street who might catch sight of the title of a book they're carrying (such as this one).

Other people's *thoughts* cannot affect you. Summon up that knowledge whenever you become aware that you are reacting to someone else's opinion of you—or more likely, what you *think* someone's opinion is.

YOU'VE GOT MORE THAN YOU THINK

The fact that you don't have everything you want, or even that you truly need, doesn't mean that you have nothing. When you've come to focus obsessively on your lack of money, your debts, pain, and the other consequences of underearning, it's as if a filter has been placed over your eyes, and all the things you have and all that is good in your life fade out and then disappear. You no longer see anything but deprivation. You no longer see anything but the problems your underearning has caused, and they become exaggerated and monstrous.

This happened to me in the last year of my debting. It progressed steadily until my life seemed composed almost entirely of deprivation, lack, and pressure.

I remember vividly an afternoon I was out walking with a friend. She stopped short and said, "Do you know what you just did?"

I said, "No. What?"

"I said, 'Look at the way the sun is coloring the clouds. Isn't that beautiful?' And you looked up for about half a second and said, 'Yeah,' and then you looked back down and said, 'I don't know what the hell I'm going to do. I've got a cap falling out, but I don't have the money to go to the dentist. I can't even make the rent next week.' Every time I've seen you in the last few months, all you've talked about is bills and money."

And she was right.

There was much about my life that was positive and good then, but I had lost sight of nearly all of it. I had, for example, largely recovered from an unexpected and painful divorce. I had two healthy and fine sons whom I loved and who loved me. I was living in Greenwich Village, which is a pleasant place to live. I had good friends. I was in better physical condition than I'd been in for years. I had a well-developed talent that I could exercise as both a craft and an art. I'd achieved a fair amount of popular and critical success over the years and my professional reputation was strong. I had a good relationship with an attractive and emotionally generous woman. . . .

No matter how pressured or impoverished you perceive yourself to be, realize that you have much, much more in your life that is good and pleasurable—right now—than you've led yourself to believe. Here is a simple but effective way to begin to reverse this perception of lack and deprivation, to show it up for the distortion it really is.

Sit down with a pad of paper. Across the top write, *Things in My Life for Which I Am Grateful.* Or, *Things in My Life I Appreciate and Enjoy.*

Now list everything you can think of.

Some people nearly gag over this idea.

"How can I do that when I'm in so much pain, when there's so much I don't have, or so much I've lost, when everyone else has so much more than I do!"

That's the point. To say that you're too worried and depressed over the lack of money in your life to make such a list, that you'll have to wait until you feel better, is to put the cart before the horse. It's making the list that will help to improve your emotions, to clear your vision, and, as a consequence, begin to improve the quality of your entire life.

Some of the things a "Gratitude List" might include are:

- I'm healthy
- My kids are great
- My stereo
- My dog
- I play a great game of tennis
- My husband loves me
- My library
- The house
- I'm good-looking
- My friends
- My computer
- The high ceilings in my apartment
- My camera
- The gym
- The oak tree
- My firm mattress
- My lover
- My jewelry
- The dishwasher
- My camping gear
- I dance well
- The antique pitcher
- My answering machine

At intervals of six months or so, make out a new list. This will help you to become, and remain, more aware of all that is good and valuable in your life and help to prevent you from slipping into gloom and self-pity.

MIRROR, MIRROR, ON THE WALL

We're going to look into a mirror. Not to ask who's the fairest but simply to get an honest look at ourself as an underearner.

Sit back and become comfortable. Breathe. Relax. Remind yourself that right now, today, you are perfectly all right.

On your pad, write the heading *Underearning.* Beneath it, list all the ways you can think of in which you actively or passively underearned over the last twelve months. (Don't bother classifying them; the purpose here is to help you *see* the ways rather than to divide them.)

For example:

- Sought work for which I wasn't qualified.
- Spent a lot of time on projects that weren't going to make me much money [if self-employed].
- Incurred heavy expenses.
- Told a prospective client I didn't know how to do what he wanted to hire me for.
- Exhausted myself during nonworking hours.
- Refused to work.
- Gave more time to my job than I was being paid to give.
- Quit without having a new source of income.
- Remained in a job that didn't pay enough to meet my needs or that paid me just barely enough.
- Was repeatedly late to work, frustrating my employer and jeopardizing my position.
- Took frequent mornings, afternoons, or even entire days off [if self-employed].
- Failed to ask for help or advice.
- Spent money I didn't have [by using a credit

card, going into my overdraft privilege, and the like].

- Let other people support me.
- Failed to use my abilities or time in an income-producing way.

-

When you're finished with this list, draw a line under it. Now make a second list. Here, write down all the ways in which other people you know underearn: set low fees, for example, insist on getting things their own way, continue to employ unproductive employees. Now get creative and add every other way you can think of: claiming that emotional problems prevent one from working, arguing constantly with co-workers and supervisors which results in never being promoted, not honoring commitments.

Take a good look at these lists. They're a lot longer than you would have imagined, aren't they? And they all add up to the same thing—underearning. After you've done this, take a break before going on to the next technique.

IS THAT LAND I SEE?

This is another discovery process. Pick up your pad and pen again. Breathe in, breathe out. Let your body relax. At the top of your pad write:

Emotions

Now, list five emotions you have about money. Don't spend a lot of time searching within or debating with yourself. Just be open. The first five that come to mind will be fine.

When you're finished, write the heading:

Statements

Here, list the first seven declarative statements that come into your mind about money. A declarative statement is a simple statement of fact, or belief. Keep them short. For example, "There's never enough of it." Or: "I don't know what to do with it."

Don't refer to emotions directly, as in: "I feel bad because there's never enough of it." You've already listed your emotions about money. Here we're sticking to simple statements of fact or belief.

Make these lists before you read any further. Reread the two paragraphs above to fix them in your mind—five emotions, seven declarative statements—then pick up your pen and pad, take a breath, relax, and make the lists.

Make them now. . . .

All finished? Good.

Take another breath, exhale, and relax.

Now look back over the emotions you put down. This list reveals to you what your primary *feelings* are about money, possibly allowing you to see them with clarity for the first time.

Now look over the declarative statements you put down. This list reveals to you your major beliefs about money, and about yourself in relationship to money—again, possibly with clarity for the first time.

What's likely, if you are an underearner, is that nearly all the emotions and declarative statements you put down were negative. Here, to illustrate, are the lists created by Tony, a forty-three-year-old furniture designer:

Emotions

1. Rage
2. Frustration

3. Despair
4. Longing
5. Sadness

Statements

1. There's never enough.
2. I try and try, but nothing ever works out.
3. I don't know what to do.
4. I want to scream at people with money.
5. Life is not fair.
6. I'm too old, too worn out to make it.
7. It's hopeless—I can't make enough.

When negative beliefs are backed up by powerful negative emotions, they tend to be self-fulfilling, to create their own reality in your life. That is why it's important for you to know what is really going on within you. Ruled by such beliefs—but only partly aware of them, or even not at all—you will have a difficult time liberating yourself from underearning.

All right, you might reasonably ask, so now that we know what the emotions are, what do we do about them?

There are many techniques and processes that can help you transform such beliefs into more positive ones or at least to neutralize their impact on you. We'll discuss several in this chapter, and more in later ones.

The first is to begin with possibilities that originate within our own selves. We are wiser than we think, once we grow quiet; we intuitively know more of what would be good for us and helpful to us than we suppose.

Turn to a new page on your pad. Breathe, relax.

Write the heading:

Things I Could Do to Change My Emotions

Under this heading, list seven things you could do to change your emotions about money. Let your imagination run free: You don't *have* to do any of these. The point is only to show yourself that there *are* ways to change, ways you never even realized or considered before. Some of your ideas will be more desirable than others.

When you're finished, breathe, exhale, and relax.

Now write the heading:

Things I Could Do to Change My Beliefs

Here, write down ten things you could do to change your beliefs or attitudes about money, or about yourself in relationship to money. (There may be some overlap in these two lists. That's fine.)

Again, let your imagination run free. Part of Prospering involves a change in consciousness. Here, and in other exercises, you'll be breaking through perceptual barriers that you or someone else placed in your way a long time ago, eliminating old restrictions in your thinking, and striking out toward new and expanding horizons. This change has already begun: You don't look upon yourself and money now in quite the same way you did before you opened this book, do you? The process will escalate as you move through the following chapters and as you work this program.

Complete the lists now.

Finished? Good. Here are the lists Tony made:

Things I Could Do to Change My Emotions

1. Make more money
2. Meditate

3. Talk to people who don't underearn
4. Talk to people who have freed themselves from underearning
5. Watch comedy shows
6. Read spiritual literature
7. Have a lot of sex

Things I Could Do to Change My Beliefs

1. Go into therapy
2. Work the Twelve Steps on money
3. Take a vacation
4. Go fishing
5. Learn something about money
6. Join the Industrial Design Society
7. Write affirmations*
8. Take responsibility for my own situation—yhhagg!
9. Give up and admit that I don't know what the hell I'm doing
10. Eat pizza. (Say what?)

Tony's lists were just that—Tony's lists. They were *his* ideas, some more effective than others, some more appealing than others. Making the lists was an important early step for him. They gave him a clearer vision of himself with money than he'd ever had before, and offered some practical ways for him to begin bringing about constructive change.

Tony's lists are included here only to serve as a model. It's

---

* An affirmation is a strong positive thought that one implants in the subconscious with the intention of producing a healthy change in attitudes and perceptions. Affirmations, intelligently used, are specific and powerful vehicles of change. Methods of working with them are described in some of the books that appear in "For Further Reading," at the end of this book.

important for you to create your own lists, out of your own being, in response to your own needs. Write out a new set every six months. You will have changed during that time, and keeping current with yourself will help you take advantage of your new strengths and to recognize other areas in which it would be useful for you to work.

QUALITY SUFFERING

Worry and fret never swayed a single decision in your favor, paid off a penny of your debt, or brought in a dollar's worth of income. Neither did fear, despair, or raking yourself over the coals. All they've ever done is make you unhappier. So what's the point?

Go to a movie. Have dinner with a friend. Listen to music. Read a book. Enjoy yourself.

Impossible, you say. I need to worry. I need to experience terror. I need to beat myself up.

Okay. Maybe you can give that up in time. But for now, since you're going to do it anyway, let's not leave it to chance and random circumstance. Let's formalize it—let's do it right.

Pick a time. For some reason, people who do this seem to favor either 11:45 A.M. or 3:30 P.M. Maybe so it doesn't interfere with lunch or the rest of the day.

Give it five minutes. Five *real* minutes. Don't shirk or use halfway measures—this is serious stuff. We're going to bury you at the bottom of the dungheap of the universe.

Okay? Get ready. Take a deep breath—we want to put a lot of energy into this. Now . . . Go!

Weep and wail. Shudder with fear. Convulse with terror. Moan with despair. That's it! Tear yourself apart. Scream at yourself. Tell yourself what a worthless, sniveling, weak-willed, crummy, rotten piece of human junk you are. Pour it on! Quake with helplessness. Cry out in the face of doom. Heap ashes and dust upon your head. Grovel. Shriek. Condemn. Kick the living daylights out of yourself!

All finished?

Good. You have now fulfilled all your moral and ethical obligation to suffer. You can return to your day again and finish it in a humane and happy fashion.

If you really wish to suffer or think you ought to, then do so in this fashion from here on. Five minutes a day, at a regularly appointed hour. For the rest of the time, be good to yourself—relax, play, do what you enjoy doing.

LET ME COUNT THE WAYS

This technique is to help you think outward in new and innovative ways. It has three parts. You can do it now or later. (And if you've actually worked with the previous techniques such as Mirror, Mirror, on the Wall and Is That Land I See? rather than simply read them, it's probably best to give yourself some respite here and defer this one till later. Do it sometime within the next two weeks, and then as many times afterward as you'd like.)

Sit down with your pen and pad. Write the heading, 100 Ways I Could Bring More Money In.

Under it, list one hundred ways you could do just that— from the realistic to the fanciful, even the farcical. Remember: You don't *have* to do any of these. Let your imagination run free. Be as wild and improbable as you can. You'll discover that one idea triggers another. To your surprise, you'll probably find that in only ten or twenty minutes you will come up with many more ideas than you would have thought possible.

Not all of these ideas will be feasible, of course, especially if you truly have been thinking in a zany way. Some will be useless or actions you would never take under any circumstances. That's fine—the point is to get down as many of them as possible. If I list one hundred actions, out of which only ten prove useful, I've still shown myself ten more possibilities than I would have if I'd simply sat around wishing things were different. It's opening up your thinking that counts.

Your list might look something like this:

100 Ways I Could Bring More Money In

1. Baby-sit
2. Rob a bank
3. Go into management
4. Ask for a raise
5. Work Saturdays
7. Write annual reports
8. Move to another city
9. Change jobs
10. Finish my college degree . . .

If you can't come up with a hundred, don't worry. Just do as many as you can and come back to the list later, in a day or two.

Now turn to a new page on your pad. At the top, write, *50 Ways I Could Cut Expenses.*

Cutting expenses is *not* a desirable tactic for an underearner in the long run. In fact, it can be damaging—an attempt to solve the problem by shrinking your life to match an insufficient income rather than by increasing your income. But in the short run, used judiciously, it can help you avoid new debt. (Incurring debt, of course, is deadly: *Nothing* enables an underearner to continue underearning as effectively as incurring unsecured debt.)

Your list might look something like the example below. Remember that except for an occasional item like the Spending Record, most of the entries will be temporary measures:

50 Ways I Could Cut Expenses

1. Iron my own shirts
2. Brown-bag lunch to work a couple of days
3. Write letters instead of making long-distance calls
4. Carpool
5. Move to a more economical apartment
6. Paint the house ourselves
7. Cook dinner for my date at home, rather than taking her/him out
8. Keep a Spending Record
9. Rent a video instead of taking the family to a movie
10. Use community facilities rather than a private health club . . .

Now turn to a new page. On it, write the final heading, *Ways I Could Get Something I Need Without Debting.*

First, put down general ways you could get things you need without debting. Then select certain items or services for which a need might rise without warning—such as a car repair—and come up with actions you could take to fill that need without debting.

The list below contains some suggestions. Keep in mind that as you progress, you'll be operating out of steadily increasing income.

Ways I Could Get Something I Need Without Debting.

General

- Review the necessity of each expenditure with scrupulous honesty. If I don't absolutely *need* to make it, defer it till a later date.
- Empty the container into which I toss my loose change. [For most people, this gives them an immediate $20 to $200.]
- Liquidate an asset such as a stock certificate or bond, even if I take a loss on it.
- Begin building a contingency fund, no matter how little I can contribute to it each week.
- Barter—my expertise in any area in exchange for someone else's I need.* [For example, clerical work in your doctor's office for his services; your legal skills for someone else's carpentry skills.]
- Secure a loan by giving the lender collateral to hold until I pay her back: skis, a CD player, a bicycle, a piece of art.
- Sell something I own, such as a piece of clothing, furniture, or art, or a set of silverware that I don't really need or to which I'm not deeply attached . . .

Specific: Car Repair

1. What is my *real* need? [In this case, probably transportation. Getting the car repaired is only

---

* In general, barter is *not* a good idea for an underearner. It reinforces the idea that you can't earn enough to pay for what you need or want. But it is always preferable to debting.

a way to fill that need.] How else could I fill it?

2. Borrow a car from a friend or relative
3. Rent a car for a while
4. Take public transportation
5. Ride with friends
6. Fix it myself
7. Any technique from the "General" ways, such as bartering or selling something
8. Have the work done in stages I can afford . . .

As you liberate yourself from underearning, you'll turn to tactics such as these less and less, and eventually discard them altogether. But they can be potent in the short run.

COMMITMENT AND COMMONPLACE MIRACLES

It is commitment that leads to innovation, recognition of opportunity, and empowerment—not the other way around. First comes the commitment, the rest follows from that.

A commitment to become free of underearning—not a wish or vague desire, but a *commitment*—shifts you into a life of increasing options and alternatives, where, as time passes and you gain experience, you begin to understand that there are very few limits except those that you impose upon yourself.

As you take positive action, positive results appear, frequently in unexpected ways and often continuing to reverberate over an extended period, sometimes long after the original action has been forgotten, and in a fashion wholly unimagined at the time.

As you replace old and distorted beliefs with new and healthy ones, clarity increases, emotions lift. As you assume control of your life, the fear begins to recede. As you emerge from underearning, the pain falls away. As you become self-reliant, your sense of well-being burgeons.

All these—the events and quality of your life, the influxes of money—are miracles, in the original sense of the word, wondrous happenings. And they do indeed become commonplace.

5.

PROCEEDING

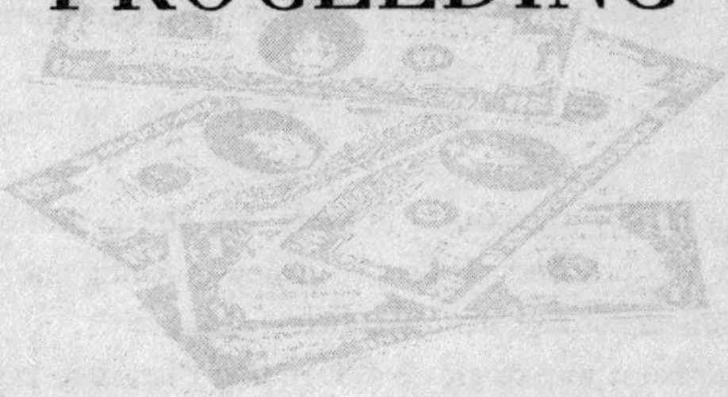

THIS CHAPTER AND THE NEXT CONTAIN PRACTICAL TECHNIQUES and strategies for freeing yourself from underearning. Is each vital? No, not in the sense of the three *Do-Nots* (do not incur debt, do not take work that pays you less than you need, and do not say no to money). Anyone might ignore one or even a few of these techniques and not jeopardize his liberation. But it is *in aggregate*, practiced as part of an integrated program, that they have their greatest impact. I consider each important; it would not be here otherwise. So I urge you to work with them all; they can only make your recovery richer, more joyful, and more satisfying. At a minimum, pick three from this chapter. If they are actions, take them; if they are techniques, begin to practice them.

THE SPENDING PLAN

The Spending Plan is a powerful tool. It helps you match your income to your expenses. It allows you to exercise options and make informed choices.

The Spending Plan is *not* a budget. It is a set of guidelines to point you in the direction you wish to go. There's a world of psychological difference between the two.

Ask yourself: "How do I plan to spend my money this weekend?"

Now ask: "How am I going to budget my money this weekend?"

They're not the same. Budgets are stern, authoritarian. Plans are flexible. Budgets lead to penny-pinching and deprivation. Plans encourage action and increase.

The easiest way to create a Spending Plan is to expand on the form you're already using for your Spending Record. Get a blank copy of your record to use as a model. On a separate piece of paper, draw up a new form, altering the old one in this fashion:

1. Change the name of the last vertical column on the right from *Total* to *Actual*.
2. Add a new vertical column to the right of that one and give it the heading, *Plan*.
3. Add a final vertical column to the right of the Plan column and mark this one + *or* −, which indicates plus or minus.

A simple example appears on the next page.

How to Use It

The purpose of the Spending Plan is to help you plan your expenses for the coming month. Let's say you're working with a net income of $2,000. Get out last month's Spending Record, which lists the totals you actually did spend last month

SPENDING PLAN FOR AUGUST							
Week	1	2	3	4	Actual	Plan	+ or −
Rent							
Food							
Clothes							
Entertainment							
Gas & Electricity							
Laundry							
Medical							
Papers & Magazines							
Telephone							
Transportation							
Totals:							

in each of your categories. These amounts are your starting point.

Think about these figures, one category at a time. Does it seem like you spent too much in this category, or maybe not enough? Pick what you think is a reasonable figure, given your income and other expenses, and enter it in the Plan column. Go through each of your categories in this fashion.

Let's say you've finished that, and that your projected expenses total $100 more than your $2,000 income. Something has to change. You'll have to sell something, put in overtime, or find some other way to get your income up to $2,100 for the month; or you could cut expenses by $100. You'll have to do one or the other. Otherwise, if you lived up to the letter of your Spending Plan, you would debt. You can't make $2,000 and spend $2,100 without debting—and incurring new unsecured debt, remember, is lethal to underearners.

(You *could* make up the shortfall by using money from your contingency fund or savings. That would not be debt. Still, done with any regularity, it would be underearning— repeatedly gaining less income than you need. And unchecked, it will inevitably lead to debt.)

At the end of the month use the last three columns in your combination plan-and-record to measure how well you did and help you formulate your new plan for the coming month. To do this, add up the weekly totals in each category to arrive at a monthly total. Enter that figure in the Actual column. Now compare the Actual entry with the Plan entry. Enter the difference in the + or − column, which represents how much more you spent than you had planned to (+, or plus), or how much less (−, or minus). To simplify, round off the amounts in the last three columns to the nearest dollar. For example:

Week	1	2	3	4	Actual	Plan	+ or −
Clothes	31.76	12.45	91.67	12.00	148	65	+83

In this example, you had planned to spend $65 on clothes last month. But you actually spent $148. So you entered +83 in the + or − column, indicating that you went over your plan for this category by $83. This entry will now help you decide how much you want to spend in the category this coming month. You may, for example, want to compensate for over- spending on clothes last month by spending nothing at all on clothes this month, or by keeping the amount to $10 or $15. Follow this procedure with each of your categories, making whatever adjustments you think appropriate.

The Spending Plan provides you with absolute clarity about what is going on with your money, and a means through which you can begin taking control of it. Working with a

Spending Plan is nearly always essential in freeing yourself from underearning.

Don't put off making one. Do it as soon as you have completed one full month of the Spending Record, which you will use as a guide. When you plan your expenses, remember that their total for the month should not exceed the total of your income, not even by ten dollars. If you plan to spend ten dollars more than you make, and you do spend that, there is only one possible result—debt. And one day at a time, as a fundamental part of Prospering, you don't debt anymore.

Work with the Spending Plan every month for six months. Then decide if you wish to continue with it. (Most people do.)

IT LOOKS LIKE THIS

Sometime within the next seven days, write out a description of your ideal relationship with money—not what you think an ideal relationship *ought* to be but what it would *actually* be for you. It's important for you to have a clear picture of this. This clarity will help you make choices and take actions that are more likely to serve your best interests. Keep the description simple, no more than two or three paragraphs.

What would having made friends with money *feel* like— would you be relaxed, joyful, something else? What would it *be* like—would you have freedom, responsibility, would it change the quality or activity of your days? How would you act— differently from now? What would you *do*?

As an alternative, you might simply want to list ten descriptive points.

To complete the exercise, sit down with a trusted friend. Explain to him that the only thing you wish to accomplish is to share with another human being a description of what your ideal relationship with money would be. Ask him not to comment—not to say, "Gee, that's terrific," or "I wouldn't do it that way," or anything else—but only to listen, and then to acknowledge that he has heard by saying simply, "Thank you."

This sharing of our ideal relationship with money with another person helps break the fearsome isolation and secretiveness that underearners often feel, makes the vision of that ideal relationship more real to us, and can provide a sense of well-being and intimacy.

ASK FOR MORE

Request a raise, raise your rates. Sometimes freeing yourself from underearning is not a matter of changing jobs, doing different work, or taking similar actions (although these may be helpful) but simply of being paid more for what you already do, and for the same number of hours you're already doing it. Larry, who writes mystery novels, says, "It takes the same amount of time and energy to write a book for five thousand dollars as it does to write one for fifty thousand dollars."

Underearners nearly always undervalue and underprice themselves.

Gloria, an executive assistant, didn't just ask for a raise, she *campaigned* for it. First she surveyed salaries in her field, finding that hers was about average. Then she wrote a two-page memo. On the first page she cited her previous excellent service, listed her strengths, and offered a procedural suggestion that she thought would improve interoffice communication—to demonstrate her commitment to the company, her interest in it, and value to it. On the second page she summarized in a short paragraph her expenses and obligations, listed her take-home pay, and pointed out that there was only a marginal difference between income and outgo. Then she wrote a cover letter requesting a raise, stating a specific figure (which she knew brought her close to the top in her field but did not exceed it) and drawing attention to her supporting memo.

She got the raise.

Gloria's employer, of course, could have offered her less than she'd asked for, or even said no altogether. In that case, Gloria would have had to think about what other options were available to her.

Clearly there are situations—many of them—in which people aren't going to get a raise no matter how many times they ask: the military, civil service, corporations with clearly defined pay levels, union shops, maybe even the deli around the corner, or an employer who simply can't or won't pay more, for whatever reason.

Some years ago I was talking with a newspaper editor about a feature on debt that I was doing for his paper's magazine section. I mentioned asking for a raise as one way to bring in more money.

"If I did that here," he said with cynicism, and dolefully, "they'd just laugh at me."

And he was right. (Well, they probably wouldn't have *laughed*, but nor would they have given him a raise.)

So what do you do in such a situation? Generally, even organizations with the most rigidly structured pay scales allow for a promotion, a move into management, or some other kind of shift that will bring an increase in pay. That is one option. And you will be practicing the other parts of this program, which will provide you with more options. But in the end, if staying where you are or continuing to work in the field you have been is a function of your underearning, then sooner or later you'll have to deal with the next topic. . . .

GUESS I'LL BE MOSEYING ON NOW

That's what the hero used to say in old westerns, after the town had been cleaned up, the hostages rescued, or the gold returned—after the job was done.

Moseying on. Yup.

And that's what you'd better do too if you are working at a job in which you're bringing in less income than you need, or than would be beneficial, and asking for more will not change that situation. To remain there would be to continue underearning. And you cannot liberate yourself from underearning by continuing to underearn. Your *real* job has been underearning. And you have worked hard at it and been very successful at it: at repeatedly gaining less income than you needed, despite the negative emotional and practical consequences that followed.

That job is over now. One day at a time, you're through with underearning. So it's time to be moseying on—toward work that will pay you enough to meet your needs in a humane fashion.

Much easier said than done, right?

Sure. Nevertheless, you're going to have to do it if you wish to free yourself from underearning. Underearning does not cease with underearning. It can't.

Does that mean you should just up and quit your job? Not unless you can walk out of it directly into a new and satisfactory one tomorrow morning. Otherwise, you'd just sink more deeply into underearning, begin bringing in even *less* than you are now, which wasn't enough in the first place.

The way to proceed is this:

1. Observe scrupulously the three *Do Nots:* Do not incur any new unsecured debt. Do not take work that pays you less than you need. Do not say no to money.
2. Begin practicing the other techniques and concepts of this program.
3. Search for a job that will pay you enough to meet all your needs in a humane fashion.
4. When you find one that will, and you like it, take it.

For many people, this is a simple process, once they become aware of their disposition to underearn. For others, depending upon their occupation and where they live, it is more difficult. But everyone *can* do it. In some cases, finding the right job or the right kind of work might mean returning to school, getting special training, moving to another city, or any number of tasks to perform or obstacles to overcome. But each task can be completed, each obstacle overcome—if you are committed to your liberation, if, as the principal book of Alcoholics Anonymous puts it, you are "willing to go to any length to get it." "Halfway measures," the same book says, "availed us nothing."

Time to be moseying on now.

MAKING ROOM FOR THE NEW

If you've been underearning for any length of time, a fair amount of what fills your life—clothes, kitchen equipment, furniture—can have become worn out, flawed, and second-rate. You may not be aware of this; you may have only a vague sense of tawdriness or insufficiency. Or if you are aware of it, you may think there's nothing you can do because you lack the money to replace something, or you tell yourself it's still serviceable, that you can make do with it. The result is blockage: Everything stays the same.

This practice is both an actual letting-go—a releasing of your grip upon something, a ceasing to cling to it—and a symbolic representation of your becoming free of underearning, of making room in your life for a new and better way of doing things to enter.

Pick a drawer, a bureau, a closet, or even an entire room in your apartment or house. Evaluate every single article within that space, from an old tie to a television set. Ask yourself: Do I really need this? Do I enjoy and take pleasure from it? If you cannot answer yes to at least one of these questions, then get rid of the item—give it away, sell it, or throw it out. Do so consciously, deliberately, as both metaphor and fact, in the faith and confidence that you are creating an empty space in your life into which—even if you cannot imagine how at the moment—will flow the new, the more desirable, and the more pleasing.

Elizabeth, a secretary, purged her apartment of every article of clothing that didn't make her feel wonderful to wear. She had an accumulation of nearly fifteen years, going all the way back to high school. Most of it went out. For her this was a courageous act, since at the time she was able to allot only forty dollars a month to buying new clothes. She even needed the company of a friend when she did it, to keep her fear at bay. Now, fourteen months later, she has a new wardrobe that is more than sufficient to cover all her needs, and she enjoys every piece in it, feels good about herself whenever she dresses.

It's best to begin with this technique on a small scale. You might, for example, want to go through your shirts or sweaters, culling out and divesting yourself of all but those you truly need or enjoy. As you gain confidence that you are not going to end up living in lack, that the new and more pleasing will indeed enter the empty space you have created, you can begin to practice the technique on increasing levels of significance, perhaps even in other areas of your life—with abusive clients, for example, or unsatisfactory relationships.

READ: *How to Get Out of Debt, Stay Out of Debt & Live Prosperously*

I debated a long uncomfortable time over whether or not to include this tool. I didn't want to appear shamelessly self-promoting. (I wrote the book.) In the end, I based my decision on two facts: that my reluctance to do so was probably a function of my own compulsion to underearn, and that if someone else had written it, I wouldn't hesitate to recommend it here. It is a valuable tool for anyone working to free himself or herself from underearning.

Hillel, a first-century Jewish scholar and teacher from Babylon, wrote: "If I am not for myself, who will be? If I am only for myself, what am I? If not now, when?"

Attentive to all three questions, I include the book.

INTRODUCING (AHEM) THE NEW, IMPROVED ME

"When I'm inside my own head," says Harry, a chef, "I'm behind enemy lines." What he means is that sitting alone with his own thoughts doesn't help him—they are depressed thoughts, fearful thoughts, the thoughts of an underearner. He means that he can't simply *think* his way out of underearning, or out of the low self-esteem that is part of his underearning, and into feeling better about himself.

So how *does* one improve one's self-image, lift one's self-esteem? Many parts of Prospering address that. Here, we're going to make only a couple of observations and offer a single technique.

First, as you integrate the concepts of Prospering into your consciousness and practice its techniques, you will automatically begin to feel better about yourself. Second, therapy may be helpful. And third, working the Twelve Steps, which are discussed in Chapters 8 and 9, will have a powerful positive impact.

Finally, a technique: One of the simplest and most effective ways to lift your self-esteem is by doing estimable—or *esteemable*—acts.

Write down a number of things you could do for which you would respect or admire yourself. Don't include anything you would dislike or even hate doing just because you think it's something you ought to do, that would be socially or spiritually virtuous. Do *not* make this list a mechanism of potential failure—include only acts you would actually consider doing. These don't have to be large or momentous. Smiling at a child on the street might be one. Helping to comfort someone who is upset, another. Or perhaps choosing not to exaggerate a story you're telling about something you did or that happened to you. If appropriate, you *could* volunteer time at a shelter for the homeless or reading to shut-ins at a hospital (assuming you don't have an underearner's history of giving away your time). Just be careful to pick actions for which you *truly* would admire or respect yourself and that you *truly* might be willing to do.

Then, little by little, undertake some of them. As time passes, new ideas will occur to you, and as your self-esteem and sense of worth begin to rise as a consequence of these actions—as both will—you will probably integrate some of them into your life on a daily basis. And the estimable acts, from tiny to large, and your self-esteem and sense of worth will interact with and feed and nurture each other in growing reciprocity.

Check in with yourself about this at the end of each month; see how you feel, what you might like to do in the coming month. Do so for a year, then decide if you wish to continue.

EVEN THE LONE RANGER HAD TONTO

Prospering, as a program, will in itself, if you adhere to it, enable you to free yourself from underearning. But you may find that it is easier and more effective to practice it in the context of a support group. People in trouble with underearning often feel a keen sense of isolation. They speak to no one about it, they feel cut off and alone. This is painful in itself, and leads to a sense of hopelessness.

A support group is a powerful tool. It provides access to a large body of experience, strength, and hope that would not otherwise be available. It offers encouragement, a feeling of community, a healthy perspective on distorted attitudes and perceptions, and a sharing of ideas, information, and techniques. At first, many balk at the idea of joining such a group. Pride comes into play, embarrassment, shame, anger.

"I'm not weak," you might say. "I can do it by myself."

Yes, you can. In fact, you'll have to. No one else could even if they wanted to. A support group offers you help, but *you're* the one who has to do the job. Joining a group is not a sign of weakness—just the opposite: It manifests courage and strength, since it flies right in the face of fear, of pride, and is an act of commitment to yourself.

"I don't want to be told what to do."

There are no authority figures in a good support group. It is a community of equals who have come together to solve their common problem and who simply share their experience, strength, and hope with each other.

"I'd be too afraid. I could never talk about this."

That is both a result and a cause of your problem with underearning. Continued isolation only intensifies it. No one ever walked into a support group eager to begin talking about his situation or without apprehension and reluctance. At first, many simply listen. In time, most begin to speak. Inevitably, they find it a relief.

"I'd be humiliated if I ran into someone I know."

Why? Everyone is there for precisely the same reason. They are no different from you, or you from them. Your imagined embarrassment stems from the belief that you've done something wrong, that you're weak-willed or incapable. That belief itself is part of the problem.

Debtors Anonymous

Debtors Anonymous (DA) as a whole remains the best and most effective support group there is for people who are in debt, although individual chapters within the organization are sometimes unclear or become stalled in areas that have little to do with debt. Its members have been dealing directly and successfully with debt for more than a decade and a half now. It is a self-help organization that has no dues or fees, with each chapter functioning independently but linked together through the organization's general administration arm.

The focus in DA is on recovery from debt, not from underearning. (The only requirement for membership is a desire to stop incurring unsecured debt.) But some members believe that it is valid to discuss in DA what they are now beginning to perceive as their problem with underearning, since that underlay much of their original debting and since continuing to underearn puts them at risk of incurring new debt.

Debtors Anonymous is well established and growing rapidly, but is not yet functioning in all parts of the country. If you are a debtor who wishes help with overcoming debt and DA is not available in your area, you might consider founding a chapter there. The program will help you do it. Write to:

> Debtors Anonymous—General Service Board
> Box 400
> Grand Central Station
> New York, NY 10163-0400

Or . . .

Alternatively, you may want to put together a support group of your own. If so, begin by discreetly seeking out others who have a problem with underearning. You can find them through a trusted friend, your therapist, your doctor or cleric, through other self-help programs, or similar avenues.

Schedule a weekly meeting of an hour to an hour and a half together. Use the material in this book as subject matter for discussion. Share your experiences, difficulties, and successes with each other.

It may seem awkward at first, but you'll feel easier as time passes, and you'll find that it's of tremendous value.

DIVERSIFICATION

Diversification is a time-honored financial principle. To diversify means to spread over several areas, to introduce variety. Corporations do it by entering multiple arenas of activity or making different kinds of products. Investors do it by buying several stocks instead of just one. The primary advantage of diversifying is that it minimizes the risk of loss—basically, it is a practical application of the old saw, "Don't put all your eggs in one basket."

Diversifying in *your* life—your earning life—can provide you with the same advantage, can minimize the damage that you might otherwise sustain in a setback such as being laid off or losing a client. It can also generate new opportunities for you and maximize your ability to take advantage of them.

Diversifying was part of my own liberation from underearning. Earlier, we said that one definition of insanity is to keep doing the same thing over and over again and expect different results. Another is to keep doing over and over again something that used to work, after the context has changed, and expect it still to work. That's what I had been doing. My first step in ending this was to admit to myself that what I had been doing—writing novels, and in a particular way (selling them before I wrote them, in proposal form)—was no longer working, wasn't bringing in enough to meet my needs. Once it had, but now it wasn't. What follows is, in distilled form, the rest of the process I went through. Most of these activities were done in conjunction with or overlapped one another:

First, I asked myself: Where does the problem lie—in me, my agent, or the changes that have taken place in publishing?

The answer, I decided, was in all three.

The solution: Change agents, alter my own activities. (There was nothing I could do about publishing, which is a monolith.)

I changed agents.

It was in changing my activities that I diversified.

I began to write for magazines again (which I hadn't

done in nearly a dozen years). The money wasn't such that it offered a long-term solution, but the cash was helpful in the short run.

In books, I turned to nonfiction, drawing upon my work, research, and experience in psychology, personal transformation, and debt recovery over the past several years.

I searched myself for other marketable skills I might have. (My résumé said: "Mr. Mundis has been a novelist for twenty years." I looked in the paper; there wasn't much corporate call for novelists.)

Editing, I decided—that was a skill I possessed. So I became willing to go into an office for a while. (Here I discovered that I had an ego-investment in never having worked for anyone else, and had to overcome that.) But though I was now willing, who would hire me? I had never *worked* as an editor in my life. In fact, except for a few months right out of college, I had never worked for *anyone* in *any* capacity. But I went ahead anyway, made phone calls, sent letters—and ended up as a feature editor at *The New York Times*, where I stayed for a year and a half.

I also knew more about overcoming writer's block than anyone I'd ever met or whose work I'd ever read. Because of my own difficulties with block, I'd had to develop and employ a variety of means over the years to render it harmless. So I put together a consultation session that would break writer's block for anyone, forever, in a single afternoon and establish for them a productive and reliable working schedule. The first year, that consulting brought in fifteen percent of my gross income.

Next, I adapted the block-breaking material into a day-long seminar designed to reinvigorate corporate staff writers who were burned out, and I took that seminar into corporations and professional associations.

Then, staying with nonfiction, I wrote a book that presented step-by-step the program I used in breaking writer's block.

Shortly after, one of my block-breaking clients, a writer and television producer, became involved with a project for cable television and asked me to join him as a writer. I did, for six months.

I also developed a series of workshops on debt recovery and other aspects of handling money in a positive way, which I presented for corporations, private institutions, and community groups in various parts of the country. . . .

Diversification, then, is a process in which you identify the skills and abilities you possess in addition to those you use in your main occupation—or further ways to apply those you already *do* use—and then find avenues through which to turn them into income-producing activities. These skills may be related to what you normally do, as mine were, or to activities you don't usually think of as sources of income, such as those associated with a sport or a hobby. Craig, for example, a high school teacher in Minnesota, and an avid fisherman and outdoorsman, diversified by guiding parties of vacationers on fishing trips, later by creating a small business out of repairing and reconditioning fishing tackle and boats, and still later by making custom bamboo fly rods to order.

Expanding into new areas of earning will also open up unforeseen opportunities. That I began to break writer's block as a consultant, for example, eventually led to me writing for television, which I'd never done before, to writing a new nonfiction book, and to leading corporate workshops for staff writers—all of which paid well.

Diversification is not only for people who work for themselves. It's just as useful for those with a full-time job or who, like Craig, have large blocks of time free. If you're in this position, you can undertake diversification part time, as something you do one or two evenings a week or on the weekend. I'm not suggesting that you simply work more hours each week: The key is to be sure that your diversifying activities are high-paying—in the sense that they bring you, ideally, *at least* twenty-five percent more per hour than you make at your job or normal work.

These activities can be temporary, their primary purpose to bring in more money while you're still at your old—underearning—job, while looking for a new one. Or they might be activities you put in place in order to have something to fall back on in case of a layoff. Or to help you make a transition out of one occupation into another.

Melanie, a retail salesclerk for a large office supply outlet, developed a part-time business setting up and configuring equipment such as fax machines and modems for small business owners who were intimidated by the equipment or just didn't want to be bothered. From there, she branched into offering the same service to people who were buying home electronic equipment—answering machines, VCRs, and the like. Within two years, she became so successful at what had been a hesitant step toward diversification that she now works as a salesclerk at the outlet only two days a week and for herself the other three. Her income is nearly thirty percent greater than it was.

Diversifying can be a useful technique.

STICK WITH THE WINNERS

Stick with the winners. That may sound elitist or brutally Darwinian, but it isn't—it's the only principle that makes sense. To do otherwise would be simply to strengthen the power of the malady over you.

So who are the winners? People with pots of money? People who've never underearned a day in their life? People with high incomes? No. Not for our purposes. Someone who's never had a drinking problem can't help an alcoholic get sober; he has no comprehension of what alcoholism is, no *experience* of it. Thus, though he may be sympathetic and willing to help, he is at a loss as to how to do so in any truly meaningful way. Nor can the drunk on the next stool help; while he has a *lot* of experience with the problem, he has none with the solution. So also with underearning. Someone who's never had a problem with it can't help in any truly meaningful way, even if she's a whiz with money herself. And someone who's still underearning herself has experience only with the problem, not the solution.

A winner is someone who's come from the same place you're in now, who is recovering from underearning, and who has something in his or her life that you'd like in your own—joy, peace, tranquillity; enthusiasm, delight; a capacity to get up in the morning with pleasure; the ability of easy laughter. None of these people set out to free himself from underearning because of an excess of joy—each started from a bottom, from a place of pain and despair.

I already know how to underearn—I don't need any help with that. I already know how to feel despair, fear, and hopelessness, how to experience frustration, anger, and self-pity. What I *need* is to listen to people who know these things, too, but who have been able to emerge from that darkness. I need to find out *how* they did it, *what* they did. "When you want to find a job," says Eric, a hospital planner, "you don't ask someone who's been on welfare twenty years how to do it."

Where can you find the winners? Currently, nearly anyone who's freeing himself from underearning and who is *committed* to that freedom, who is willing to go to any lengths to achieve it, is a winner. In places where there are few or perhaps even no such persons, you can draw support from people you admire and respect, who have something in their lives you'd like to have in yours, and who are members of other self-help groups, especially those based on the Twelve Steps. Or you can form a support group of your own, as I mentioned before.

Finally, if you are completely isolated, if you can't find even one other recuperating underearner with whom to meet for now, then sit down once or twice a week for half an hour with this book and imagine that you and I are sitting there together, sharing our experience, strength, and hope with each other. If possible, share the fact of your recovery from underearning with one other person whom you trust, who has only your well-being at heart, and who will support you even if he or she doesn't fully understand what you're doing—so you know that you are not alone and don't have to be.

And know, in the words of Julian of Norwich, a fourteenth-century mystic, that "all shall be well and all shall be well and all manner of thing shall be well."

That it is, and they are, already.

REMAIN OPEN

Finally, remain open—open to new and unexpected possibilities of recovery. To any technique, discipline, or practice you might encounter that can help you in your liberation from underearning.

When the student is ready, goes a Zen aphorism, the teacher will appear. How does one become ready? In part by keeping oneself unobstructed and receptive, by setting aside biases and preconceptions, by being willing to listen, to consider. Who is the teacher? A person, a book, a phrase; an image, a thought, an overheard conversation. An inspiration. A television show. A lover.

We recognize the teacher only when we are open to the possibility of being taught. Wisdom can come through any agency, at any time, if we are willing to receive it.

Remain open.

6.

COUPLES AND FAMILIES

WHEN YOU'RE FREEING YOURSELF FROM UNDEREARNING IN THE context of a couple or a family, you face dynamics not encountered by people who live alone. This chapter provides techniques specifically addressing those dynamics. If you're not part of a couple or family and would like to move directly to Chapter 7, go ahead, though I suggest you read this chapter anyway; you might well find material here that you can put to good use in your own life.

There are three basic configurations possible for those who live with others: couple, family, and single-parent family. The most important point to make about all of them is that within them the basic mechanisms of liberation remain the same as for people who live alone. You can't free yourself from underearning by incurring new debt to get dental braces for your daughter any more than someone who is single can by incurring it to fly off to the islands on holiday.

Certainly the process can be more challenging when you are part of a couple or a family—and painful in ways not experienced by those who live alone. But not *extraordinarily* more challenging, nor *extraordinarily* more painful. Further, differences in temperament, experience, and other areas will make this distinction largely meaningless in many cases.

No matter who you are or what your living conditions, this is precisely how difficult your own situation is— more difficult than some, less difficult than others.

You are taller than some people, shorter than others. Freeing yourself from underearning will be harder for you than for some, easier than for others. That's the way it will always be —for you, me, and everyone else. Qualitatively, our experiences will be about the same.

But what about differences between the sexes—don't they affect the process? What differences do exist—biological, cultural, historical, perhaps even emotional and psychological— will affect the manner and style in which one frees oneself, but less so than one's personality and character will. The concepts and techniques of liberation are for *human beings*, not sexes. Underearning is no more gender specific than alcoholism is; nor is liberation from it.

This chapter is divided into four sections: Couples, Families, Single-Parent Families, and In Closing. For people with children, each is relevant.

As we said earlier, it is in *aggregate*, practiced as part of an integrated program, that the elements of Prospering have their greatest impact: If this chapter is relevant to you, then at a minimum, pick three actions or techniques from it. If they are actions, take them; if they are techniques, begin to practice them.

COUPLES

J'accuse

"It's his fault."

"Her fault."

"If she'd go to work, everything would be all right."

"If he'd get a better job, we wouldn't have these problems."

Underearners are usually very sensitive to their partner's underearning, when that partner is also an underearner (fairly common). They're certain their partner's underearning is the chief cause of the financial trouble in the relationship, that they themselves are unfairly burdened, and that if their partner would only pull his or her own weight—or even just a bit more than now—they would be all right as a couple and wouldn't have these problems.

It may be true that your partner *does* have a problem with underearning and that it *is* contributing to the difficulties in the relationship. But usually—unless the discrepancy between your incomes is immense, or your partner is a spendthrift as well as an underearner—you would scarcely notice this or be much bothered by it if you weren't an underearner yourself. It is your own fear, which stems from your own underearning, that sensitizes you to your partner's underearning.

Sometimes an underearner uses his partner's underearning as camouflage for his own or to fuel his denial that *he* has a problem with underearning. This is especially true when his partner's underearning is more vivid or severe than his own. It's possible that you think you've been reading this book for your partner's benefit, nodding your head as you recognize her on this page or that or hoping he'll be able to see the problem for himself once you tell him about it or give him the book.

Uh-huh.

The fact is, you're not likely to have picked up this book or to have read this far in it if you weren't an underearner yourself. It's *possible*, but not likely. Here is a truth:

You can never force, or cause, anyone else to recover from underearning.

You can only get free of it yourself. What *can* happen is that when you undertake to liberate yourself, then your partner, after some time in which to observe the changes in your life, eventually will too. (We'll discuss your options when this is not the case in the last section of this chapter.)

In another scenario, your partner may not be an underearner at all, may bring in a perfectly adequate or even generous income. In this case, you are probably reluctant to admit to your own underearning and instead present a host of "reasons" to explain or justify why you haven't been generating enough to meet your needs. You may be depressed or angry over this or resentful of your partner, and accuse him of not being sensitive to you or understanding you.

Whatever the circumstance, money is a troublesome issue in your household, you're convinced that your partner bears the major responsibility for this problem, and you are quick to accuse her of that.

Conclave

The best way for you and your partner to begin together to form a new relationship with money is through Conclave. Conclave is a structured process that enables you to tell each other what you think or feel about yourselves and money, and about both of you together with money, without risk of fear, blame, or anger.

(It is also a potent technique to use later on to defuse

potentially explosive confrontations over money and help you instead to communicate with ease, openness, and even pleasure, and effect positive change.)

To conduct a Conclave: Decide who will go first (A), and who second (B). Agree that whoever is speaking will stick to the format of this process, and that the partner will listen attentively and respond only with: "Thank you."

Sit in chairs facing each other, close enough so that your knees are almost touching. Look directly into your partner's eyes while he or she is speaking.

The process has five parts.

In the first, A tells B the *three things* he likes *most* about *himself* with money. As A makes each statement, his partner—listening closely—acknowledges that she has heard him, understood him, and appreciates his having shared this with her by saying, "Thank you."

Only "Thank you"—nothing more, nothing less.

The process looks like this:

A: One of the things I like most about myself with money is that I'm generous with it.

B: Thank you.

A: Another thing I like most about myself with money is that I haven't incurred any new unsecured debt in nine years.

B: Thank you.

A: Another thing I like most about myself with money is that I manage it well.

B: Thank you.

Now, in the second part, A continues by telling B the *two things* he likes *least* about *himself* with money. Again, B answers only with "Thank you." For example:

A: One of the things I like least about myself with money is that I think about it too much.

B: Thank you.

A: The other thing I like least about myself with money is that sometimes I still think I don't deserve any.

B: Thank you.

Next, A tells B the *three things* he likes *best* about *them* with money. Not about her, but about *them, together*. For example:

A: One of the things I like best about us with money is that we each see ourselves as responsible for ourselves.

B: Thank you.

A: Another thing I like best about us with money is that neither one of us debts.

B: Thank you.

A: The other thing I like best about us with money is that we don't have any secrets about it that we keep from each other.

B: Thank you.

Next, A tells B the *two things* he likes *least* about *them* with money. Again, not about her—but what he likes least about *them, together*. It might look like this:

A: One thing I like least about us with money is that we sometimes get defensive or upset when we talk about it.

B: Thank you.

A: The other thing I like least about us with money is that we don't talk about it enough.

B: Thank you.

Finally, A tells B the *one thing* he would *most like to see come about* with *them* about money. Note that he isn't saying this is something he'd like to change about them but rather something he'd like to see come about—to happen, to evolve. Note also that he isn't saying this is something he'd like to see come about with her, but that he would like to see come about with them. For example:

A: The one thing I'd most like to see come about with us about money is that we become more comfortable with each other in talking about it.

B: Thank you.

That's the end of A's part.

When A concludes, both of you should take a breath, lean back, and relax. Perhaps you'd like to stretch and take another breath or two. When you're ready, begin again, this time reversing your roles: Now B goes through the process, telling A what she likes most and then least about herself with money, about them together with money, and what she would most like to see come about with them and money. After each of her statements, her partner responds only with, "Thank you."

It's important to follow the model above. The structure and phrasing are carefully designed to prevent blame or criticism from creeping in. They also emphasize what is liked most rather than least, which helps keep the focus on the positive. It's important, too, for the partner who is listening to respond with *nothing more than,* "Thank you." No comments, no argument. No agreement or disagreement. No helpful suggestions, no interested discussion. Only: "Thank you." This provides full acknowledgment of the communication and appreciation of its intimacy but prevents any possibility of judgment.

To further safeguard the process, agree beforehand that neither of you will try to discuss anything that might come up in it for at least twenty-four hours. You might want to end by giving each other a hug, and perhaps holding each other in loving silence for a minute or so.

Conclave prepares the way for you and your partner to take the next step, an important one that is detailed in the next topic. Later, Conclave can help you maintain a healthy awareness of yourself and your partner in relationship to money and of your strengths and weaknesses as a couple in handling it. Hold your first Conclave early, within a few weeks of your consciously beginning to free yourself from underearning, and then whenever else you think it might be helpful.

Now We Two Are Three

"And now we two are one . . ." goes an old wedding song.

Nice, romantic. Very loving. Spiritual. Only it doesn't work—not when money is involved and one or both partners are underearners. In fact, trying to pool your money into a communal pot in such a situation would probably be catastrophic, breeding anger, fear, jealousy, blame, resentment—and those just for openers.

The song to sing, paraphrasing Fats Domino, is: "Just honey and me, and household makes three."

Because there are *my* expenses, *your* expenses, and the *house's* expenses. The house's, or household expenses, are those we have in common, which are necessary to us as a couple and that benefit us both: rent or mortgage payment, the money we spend on food, on electricity, car payments, and the like. What is needed in any couple are three Spending Plans—one for you, one for me, and one for the house. So the next step is to address that.

The Household Spending Plan

Yours, Mine, and the House's

You've made a Spending Plan for yourself. You're enthused, you love the idea of getting free of underearning. You feel better about yourself and about us than you have for a long time. You're hopeful. Now, how do you get me to make a Spending Plan for myself?

You don't. You can't get me, or make me, do anything. What you *can* do is share your enthusiasm with me and explain in a caring, nonbelligerent way why you think it would be helpful to you, to me, and to us as a couple for me to draw up such a plan, and then hope for the best. If I resist this or any other part of Prospering, and you harp at or badger me, the situation will deteriorate and our relationship simply get worse.

But let's say for now that I do see the sense of this and do make a Spending Plan of my own. We may wish to share our plans with each other, we may not. Your plan is yours, and what you choose to do with your money is really none of my business. My plan is mine, and what I choose to do with my money is really none of your business. Each of us is entitled to privacy here if we wish it, and at least a certain amount of privacy is generally healthy.

But the house's Spending Plan is an entirely different story. That is very much *both* of our business, and it must be if we are to have any hope of positive change at all.

Drawing Up the House's Plan

Even if I refuse to draw up a Spending Plan of my own, I might still see the sense in us sitting down together to draw up one for the house, covering *our* expenses. If I don't, perhaps you can persuade me to do it anyway, as a bit of practical help I can give you in what you're doing.

(Perhaps you *can't* persuade me. Maybe I'm deeply opposed to all this—for whatever reasons—and refuse even to discuss the subject with you. What then? There are options, some happier than others, that we'll discuss later. Here, let's assume that I am willing.)

Couples vary in what they designate shared expenses as opposed to personal expenses and in how they apportion those between themselves. The first task is to list all of the *household's* expenses. The electric bill, for example, is a household expense. Your perfume is your expense; his golf shoes his expense; and each of you is responsible for your own haircuts. Here's a list of some expenses most couples consider to be household expenses:

- Cabs (if taken together)
- Car
- Children's expenses
- Gas/electricity
- Groceries
- Home equipment
- Home furnishings
- Home heating
- Home repair/maintenance
- Home supplies
- Housecleaning
- Investments
- Life insurance (if married)
- Medical insurance (if married)
- Property taxes
- Pet
- Rent/mortgage
- Telephone
- Vacation/travel
- Miscellaneous

Use or modify any of these for your own Household Spending Plan, and add any not mentioned here that you specifically need. Rank your categories in the way that seems easiest for you. Some people, for example, place the obvious ones like Rent and Groceries at the top, then list the others in alphabetical order.

Apportioning Expenses

How do you apportion household expenses honestly and fairly between you? Ideally, you and your partner would each pay fifty percent of these shared expenses. In many cases (especially in couples without children), that is what actually happens, or eventually happens. But in others it is neither reasonable nor possible. We cannot make definitive statements about this, but we can provide general guidelines. If you follow the five principles below, you'll be able to divide up your common expenses successfully.

First: Do the apportioning within the framework of this entire program, with a knowledge and understanding of all its concepts and techniques. Do it out of commitment to your recovery and with respect and regard for your partner. To help in this, don't try to draw up a Household Spending Plan until you have read through to the end of the book.

Second: Each partner's contribution should be at least equivalent to what he or she would have to spend in order to be self-supporting if living alone. (Not necessarily in the style you both are now, but in one that would be reasonable and humane; when you live with someone, your share of some expenses, such as rent, will logically be lower than what either of you would have to spend if you lived alone.)

Third: Acknowledge any legitimate discrepancy that exists between your incomes. A legitimate discrepancy is one that results from the realities of life rather than from underearning —either yours, your partner's, or both. For example: You are both underearners, both recuperating. You are a medical doctor. Your partner is a professor of English literature. You are earning four times the income he is—and can. Here, it is reasonable for you to pay a greater share of the household expenses than he does; perhaps even as high as eighty percent, especially for lifestyle choices such as vacations or dining out. (In some categories, it may be reasonable for you to pay one hundred percent.) Of course, the reverse is true too: If your partner earns four times what you do, and you are not underearning, then it's reasonable for him to be paying a larger percentage of the shared expenses.

Fourth: Factor into your Household Spending Plan the work either of you does around the house that is necessary to daily living. This might include cooking, cleaning, child-watching, lawn-mowing, house maintenance, and the like. Factor it in as a cash contribution. (How to do this will be delineated later in this chapter.)

Fifth: If necessary, use a progressive scale of apportionment —one linked to time. In this method, a given partner pays a bit more each month until he or she reaches a certain level. For example: Ellen is an underearner. Frank, her husband, is not. Their rent was $1,200 a month at the time Ellen embarked upon recovery. Frank had been paying $1,000 of that. They agreed when they drew up their Household Spending Plan that Ellen would raise her contribution to the rent by $50 each month until she was paying half of it, which took eight months to achieve.

This method can be particularly useful in situations where one partner has been underearning so severely that his or her income is practically nonexistent at the start of recovery.* It may be applied to all shared expenses or only to some. If you

---

* It also works well with an underearner who lives alone and who has been subsidized by parents up to now.

use it, be careful to avoid a timetable so slow that it becomes an instrument of enabling rather than of liberation. (I'll have more to say about personal versus shared expenses later in this chapter.)

The simplest way to make a Household Spending Plan is to keep a household spending record for a month, logging all the expenses the house incurs, then use that as a guide in creating a plan.

Matching Your Personal Plan to Your Household Plan

Reconciling your personal Spending Plan to your Household Spending Plan is relatively simple. Your personal plan should include, in addition to those categories that are strictly personal, all the household categories to which you contribute too. For example, if you contribute $600 to the household as your share of its $1,200 rent, then you *personally* are spending $600 a month on rent—and that should be noted in your personal plan. If the household spends $500 a month on groceries and your share of the house expenses is fifty percent, then you *personally* are spending $250 a month on groceries—and that should be noted in your personal plan. So also with every other household category.

It might seem simpler at first just to lump all those different expenses into one category called Household on your personal plan and enter the total you contribute to the house. But that would deprive you of clarity; you wouldn't really know where the money is going, only that it *is* going.

Here are some categories that most couples consider to be personal expenses:

- Alimony
- Books
- Cabs (if taken alone)
- Car (if it's your own)

- Charitable contributions
- Child support
- Clothes
- Cosmetics
- Dry cleaning
- Education
- Food out (if alone: fast food, diners)
- Gifts (to each other, or to personal friends)
- Haircuts/beauty salon
- Hobby
- Income taxes (if assessed beyond amount withheld; adjusted for joint-filing rates if married)
- Life insurance (if not married)
- Magazines/newspapers
- Medical (doctors, prescriptions, glasses)
- Medical insurance (if not married)
- Personal care
- Personal growth
- Professional dues
- Sport
- Therapy
- Tuition
- Union dues
- Vacation/travel (if taken alone)
- Vitamins

Particular couples may consider any of these to be a shared expense. Agreement is what matters most here.

The Rule of Three

The Rule of Three says that both partners will probably be happier, that there will be more peace in the relationship, and that liberation will be facilitated when there are three separate checking accounts and three separate savings accounts—when each partner has his own and her own personal checking account and savings account, and when the house has its own two accounts. These latter two, the household accounts, are held jointly by both partners, and all the shared expenses are paid directly out of them. This arrangement makes perfectly clear what is the household's money and what is not. It provides both partners with a sense of privacy and independence, and it helps an underearner gain a more accurate vision of his or her real circumstances.

Summit Meeting

After you've established a Household Spending Plan, schedule a series of Summit Meetings together. A Summit Meeting is a semiformal conference in which the two of you sit down together to discuss everything that is pertinent to the household's finances and make any decisions required. After you've taken care of the household's needs, each of you should be free to discuss anything with your partner about your own finances that you'd like to or about which you would like some feedback.

It's best to hold a Summit Meeting once a week for the first few months. Saturday or Sunday after breakfast is often a good time. Later, if you're comfortable with the change, you can meet on whatever schedule keeps things running smoothly. Many couples make twice-monthly meetings a regular part of their life. They're an effective way to communicate on an ongoing basis about shared expenses and any questions or problems that might arise.

The Wet Tub Discussion

Sooner or later something will come up between you and your partner about money that is particularly difficult—too charged to try to resolve in a regular Summit Meeting or deal with through a Conclave. The Wet Tub Discussion is a good way to defuse the situation. It allows you to talk the problem over with minimal rancor and helps you to find a happy and workable solution. Here's how to do it:

1. Fill a bathtub two-thirds with warm water.
2. Take off your clothes, each of you.
3. Get into the tub together facing each other.
4. Smile at each other for ten seconds.
5. Begin your discussion.

It's very difficult to become angry with someone when you're sitting naked in a tub of warm water with him or her. Many people laugh self-consciously at this suggestion at first, but nearly everyone who tries it finds that it helps them to say what they want to in a way that is neither threatening nor accusatory, that it encourages openness, and that it makes it easier for both partners to treat each other with care and affection.

Limit your tub time to about half an hour. If you can't resolve the situation in that time, set it aside till the next day, then repeat the procedure. Most situations can be cleared up in one or two sessions. Occasionally you might want to practice this technique even when you don't have anything difficult to discuss, just for the hell of it.

FAMILIES

What differentiates a couple from a family?

Children.

Children make it necessary for a couple—now a family—to address concerns that childless couples don't need to, just as those couples have to deal with issues not faced by underearners who live alone. (The fact remains, though, that families and couples cannot free themselves from underearning; only *individuals* can. While anyone's recovery will benefit the people around him, that recovery must be singular.)

Children have needs. Some of those needs are financial. Since children cannot meet those needs by themselves, then you must. Therefore, your children's financial needs are *your* financial needs—just like any others you have. And their expenses are *your* expenses—just like any others you have. There's no way around that. If you are tempted to feel uncommonly burdened by this, remember that your situation is no different from that of any other underearner: more difficult than some, less difficult than others.

Prospering has no philosophic or political opinion about how a family ought to organize itself or manage its finances. The concepts and techniques that follow are offered only as ways to help you become free of underearning.

Accord

To reach accord is to come to agreement or into harmony. It's what nations do—ideally. Sometimes they do it at summit meetings. You and your partner need to reach accord, too, over every question that either of you has concerning your children's expenses. The only *general* point to make about these expenses is that they belong in the Household Spending Plan (except, sometimes, in the case of children from a previous marriage, as we'll discuss). A simple way to deal with these expenses clearly is to create a category called Children in your Household Spending Plan, then break that down into subcategories such as Clothes, Medical, Toys, and the like.

Matters over which you and your partner need to reach accord might include situations like this: You have to pay a big chunk of your monthly income in alimony and child support —should this be reflected in the amount you are expected to contribute to household expenses? Or the reverse: You *receive* alimony and child support every month—should *this* be reflected in the amount you are expected to contribute to household expenses?

George and Sarah live together. Both work in television, and make about the same amount of money. George has two children from an earlier marriage. He pays child support for his youngest and most of the college tuition for his eldest. The accord he and Sarah reached was that she would contribute sixty percent to their shared, household expenses and he forty percent.

Richard, a data processor, is married to Gina, an organist and choirmaster. Richard, like George, pays child support, for a son from an earlier marriage. He also makes more money than Gina does or can in her field. Gina has a daughter from a previous marriage of her own, who lives with them. Their accord called for them to include Gina's daughter in their household plan, for Gina to place into the household fund the money she received in child support from her former husband, and for each of them then to contribute fifty percent of the remaining household needs.

Questions can arise about apportioning food and entertainment expenses when children from a former marriage come to visit for the weekend. There will also be issues that do not involve children but are similar in that they have no clear and immediately apparent answer that will require accord too.

Ben and Jeannine, for example, put their telephone expenses in their Household Spending Plan, as most couples do. But Jeannine liked to make long calls to old college friends in other cities, which resulted in high phone bills. Ben, who was contributing fifty-five percent of the household's expenses and who was a recuperating underearner (Jeannine was not an underearner), felt abused and taken advantage of in this. He wanted Jeannine to stop making the calls. Jeannine felt controlled and bullied. This was a source of friction between them for weeks, until they agreed to sit down together at a Summit Meeting and not to get up until they had reached accord. The accord they reached was to keep a log book next to the telephone and enter into it every long-distance number they dialed. When the bill arrived each month, they matched the numbers on it against the log book, and each paid for his or her own long-distance calls. They were both satisfied with this.

There aren't any hard and fast rules about accord—only a need to reach one over any financial issue that is divisive or that causes either of you to feel resentful or victimized. In sitting down to reach accord, do so as best you can with the spirit of the whole of Prospering in mind.

What's It Worth?

In most families, one partner puts in more time working in the household's behalf than the other, sometimes much more time. Traditionally, this has been the female partner. That is not always the case now, but it is still more true than not and probably will be for a while. For our purposes, though, which partner does this is irrelevant: What's relevant is how that fact is acknowledged.

Hours spent working in behalf of the household, or rather the *cash value* of those hours, need to be recognized as a contribution to the Household Spending Plan, one every bit as real as if the partner who worked them had written a check to the household. The best way to handle this is for you and your partner to come up with a figure that is agreeable to both of you through casual discussion. If you think it would be helpful to approach the question more formally, here are four simple guidelines you might use.

First: Begin by recognizing that your time—as the time of a human being—is neither more valuable nor less valuable than your partner's time. Your *earning power* per hour or day may be different, but the *absolute value* of that hour or day, as a unit of time, is not. Your time, as the time of a human being, is worth exactly the same as your partner's. One hour equals one hour, regardless of who works it or how much he or she can command for it on the market.

Second: Estimate the number of work-hours your household requires in order to keep functioning well. Restrict these to *true* work-hours, such as shopping, lawn-mowing, or caring for young children. Don't include time spent doing the things we all do for ourselves or for each other as a matter of course, such as picking up after ourselves or playing with our children. A simplified reckoning might look something like:

Household Requirements
Weekly

10 childcare hours
 8 shopping hours
12 cooking hours
 5 house maintenance/repair hours
11 housecleaning hours

Total: 46

In most cases, these work-hours should be considered your joint responsibility, in equal parts, regardless of how you apportion your household *cash* expenses. But that doesn't mean you have to work these hours in equal parts if you don't want to; the third guideline offers a fair way to modify a fifty-fifty contribution.

Third: If you wish not to work household hours in equal parts, the first step is to calculate the financial value of those hours. That's easy to do. Examine the want ads in your local newspaper to see what kind of wages are being offered for these services, or survey friends who hire people to do such things for them. Child care, for example, might be worth from $3 to $10 an hour depending on where you live and the care desired. Let's say that the going rate in your area is $7. Let's say you could hire someone to do your grocery shopping for you for $5 an hour. Cooking, $15. Work around the house such as painting or window-puttying, $20. Housecleaning, $10. So now we have something that looks like:

House Requirements
Weekly

10 childcare hours	@	$7	=	$70
8 shopping hours	@	5	=	40
12 cooking hours	@	15	=	180
5 repair/ maintenance hours	@	20	=	100
11 cleaning hours	@	10	=	110
			Total:	$500

Peter and Kelly have two children. Let's say, in the schedule above, that Kelly is putting in all the household hours except those spent on repair and maintenance, which Peter does. That means that Kelly—who is doing thirty-four hours of various kinds of work for the household each week, worth from $5 to $15 an hour on the market—is contributing $400 of the total $500 worth of services their household requires. Peter, who is putting in five hours a week of house repair and maintenance, which is worth $20 an hour on the market, is contributing $100 worth.

Since Peter and Kelly are each individually responsible for contributing 19.5 hours—or $250 worth—of services to the house, then Kelly is not only meeting her share but is contributing another $150 worth on top of it.

    $400 (Kelly's actual contribution)
    −250 (Kelly's responsibility)
    $150 (extra amount Kelly has contributed)

To correct this imbalance, Kelly should be given credit for having already contributed $150 in cash to the household for the week, and Peter should put in an extra $150 (since Kelly has done $150 worth of what can be considered *his* household work).

If we continue this example through the month, it would mean, since there are 4.3 weeks in a month, that Peter would contribute $645 more in cash beyond what he normally would, and Kelly $645 less ($150 per week × 4.3 weeks = $645).

If their household's monthly cash expenses are $2,000, and Peter and Kelly have apportioned those expenses equally, then each would be responsible for contributing $1,000. Each would *also* be responsible for performing 83.8 hours of household tasks per month. But Kelly has already performed not

only her own share of household work, but $645 worth of
Peter's too. Peter, therefore, will contribute $1,645 in actual
cash toward the month's expenses, and Kelly $355.

If the math here confuses you, don't worry about it. You
don't need to master this formula or any other in order to
work out a fair arrangement over household work-hours. All
that's necessary is for you to be easy and clear with each other
and to approach the process in good faith and with mutual
respect and affection. Given that, you'll be able to come up
with a good plan together.

Fourth: Should one of you utterly refuse to perform any of
the necessary household tasks at all, for any reason—from
domestic politics to arcane religious belief—there is still a
simple solution. He or she can contribute an appropriately
larger share of cash to the household, as in the example above,
or hire someone else to perform them. In the latter case, of
course, that person would pay for such help out of his or her
personal Spending Plan.

"Well, damn it, if she's not going to do any of the household work herself, then I'm not going to either!"

Okay, then you can *both* hire others to do it.

Many variations are possible here. The household might
hire people to do the housecleaning and lawn-mowing, while
the partners perform the rest of the tasks themselves—or
practically any other combination you can think of.

Swiss Family Robinson-ing It

The Swiss Family Robinson, by nineteenth-century Swiss writer
J. D. Wyss, is an adventure novel about a shipwrecked family,
children and parents, that has to pull together on the island
where they find themselves washed up, first to survive, then
finally to triumph. The story has been a favorite in Western

literature for almost two centuries. Today most people know it through the popular Walt Disney movie of 1960.

In the Swiss Family Robinson technique, you enlist your entire family into the cause of liberation and make the process of liberation, as best you can, into an adventure.

(I know: Underearning is *always* singular. But in some cases, to a limited extent, the family can be looked upon as an underearning unit, especially when both parents are underearners, or in single-parent families, which means that in some ways it can work as a unit toward liberation.)

Be honest with your children. Explain to them, according to their level of comprehension, what the situation is and what you're setting out to accomplish. Phrase this positively. Be careful not to say anything that will alarm or frighten them, especially if they're young. (And indeed there *is* nothing alarming or frightening—you're getting free of underearning now.) It's not necessary to go into detail or to talk about underearning or liberation from it. Just give them the essence: Here's where we are, here's what we want to do, and here are some of the ways we're going to do it.

If you'd like, include the children in your Summit Meetings, or some of the meetings. Whatever you do, be sure to give them a sense of real participation—of helping to plan, being able to volunteer ideas, having a vote, monitoring progress with you, and participating in resolving questions that come up.

David and Carole's children were twelve, nine, and seven when the family began to practice this technique. Together, infused with all the feeling of adventure that David and Carole could bring to it, the family divided up the household tasks, created a system to recognize and honor each other's accomplishments, met at a family Summit Meeting twice each month (with David and Carole meeting alone on alternate weeks), and made as many decisions as possible by vote.

"Carole and I felt we didn't have to lie or hide anything from the children," David says. "They understood and accepted things I never would have expected them to. Since they had a say, and knew some of the *whys*, and saw us all as a team, they didn't object much to missing out on some of the stuff their friends had or did or pitching in to help. Sometimes they were outright enthusiastic."

When you have older children in their late teens, candor is probably the only element of this technique that is helpful. How much detail you wish to go into with them will depend on you, them, and your relationship with them. But at the very least, some kind of open discussion of family finances with them—of what's possible, what isn't, and why—will be helpful.

In the early days of my recovery from debt, my discretionary money was very limited. At that time, I had my youngest son with me every other weekend. I talked with him honestly about my finances, and the fact that I was getting myself out of debt, and I shared with him some of steps I was taking to accomplish that. He understood. He joined with me in shopping and cooking, hunting through the newspapers for places to go and activities to do that we would both enjoy and that weren't costly. We had very good times together, and were close.

Could we have had equally good times, and been equally close, if I'd been able to take us to Belize for a week of scuba-diving, or out to dinner frequently, or to the theater? I like to think so. But I *know* we had good times then, and that we *were* close. And I cherish those times in memory, particularly now that he is grown up and living three thousand miles away in California. I wouldn't at all mind living one of those weekends again when we went to the farmer's market at Union Square on Saturday morning, and cooked a pot of curried rice with onions and raisins, and played board games, and took the subway up to the Broadcasting Museum on East Fifty-third Street to watch old television shows from the 1950s. I wouldn't mind it at all.

My God, Me as *Enabler*?

Be careful not to become, or continue to be, an enabler in your family. You can enable your partner to keep underearning by giving or lending him money, by paying her bills, or by putting more than your share of money into the household accounts to make up for him putting in less than his. If you're the parent of an adult child who is also an underearner, either living with you or not, you can fall into enabling her the same way.

Prospering is not about your partner getting free of underearning, or your child, or anyone else. It's about *you* getting free of it. Still, if you begin or continue to enable someone else, you are not helping him but actually causing him harm, and sooner or later your enabling will put a strain on your own liberation.

It may be hard for you to see at this point how you, as an underearner yourself, could enable someone else. But people do find ways, especially when they're getting better themselves. Most often they are motivated by compassion. They make excuses for their mate or grown child and bail him out—and then again, and again. This is not help. It is enabling.

Occasionally, enabling has a darker side. Some people are trying to buy love or approval through their enabling. Others want to keep the person they're giving money to helpless and dependent on them. Well-intentioned or not, enabling is toxic to both parties. The kindest thing you can do for an underearner is to stop shielding her from the consequences of her underearning.

SINGLE-PARENT FAMILIES

If you haven't read the sections on COUPLES and FAMI-
LIES earlier in this chapter, please go back and read them
now. Most of the material there applies to you, even if you're
the head of a single-parent family.

This section does not address single-parent families in
general—no more than the preceding sections addressed couples or families in general. Rather, it offers three techniques
for underearners who happen to be the head of a single-parent
family to use in addition to those in the other parts of Prospering. The operative description here is *underearner*, not single
parent.

The bulk of single-parent families are still headed by
women, though the number of men who head such families is
increasing. These techniques, like all the others in the book,
remain the same regardless of your sex.

Co-oping

Create a network with other heads of single-parent families.
While barter is generally counterproductive for underearners,
here it can be helpful, especially in the beginning. Trade what
you have that others in the network might want for what they
have that you need.

Clothes, furniture, and similar items that are in good condition can be passed from a household whose children have
outgrown them to another whose children are just growing
into them. Prices on everything from clothes to appliances and
automobiles can sometimes be reduced by offering to make
bulk or multiple purchases.

Three single mothers in Delray Beach, Florida, for example, who needed to replace their family automobiles, went sep-

arately to the used-car division of a dealer whom they had agreed upon. Each picked the car she wanted, negotiated the best price she could, but then declined to buy it and said she wanted to think about it. Then they returned to the dealer together—and in exchange for offering to buy all three cars were able get an additional six percent discount on each car.

Child-watching hours can often be arranged as a swap, to be repaid in kind. Out of the camaraderie that can grow in a single-parent network, people sometimes exchange professional work or services too—carpentry, dentistry, bookkeeping, nearly anything that one member specializes in and another needs.

Teaming up to rent an apartment or house and forming a kind of extended family is another form of co-oping. Jane, who had a three-year-old son, moved with Sasha, who had two daughters, fourteen and eleven, into a small house. They lived there for nearly two years, at a household cost significantly lower than what either would have had to pay alone, and each had someone with whom to share the adult tasks.

Where can you find other single parents with whom to form a network? Through your church or synagogue. Through community associations and organizations. Through men's groups or women's groups. By meeting them at playgrounds or children's events. Through community newspapers, newsletters, and building bulletin boards. In a self-help program. Through school guidance counselors, your pediatrician, and friends.

You're Entitled

You are entitled to use every resource available to you and to receive every benefit for which you're qualified.

No one likes to feel weak or dependent. Even underearners still in the grip of their affliction are unhappy and uncomfortable with having others provide them with what they need. Getting free of underearning, many find it difficult to ask for help or to accept it—thinking they ought to be able to do everything for themselves immediately, or because they fear it would mean slipping back, or because they *want* the help, which makes them feel guilty.

Here is something you need always to keep in mind: If it's not underearning, then whatever else it may be, it's not underearning.

If something you do does not involve incurring new debt, taking work that pays you less than you need, or saying no to money, then—at a threshold level—it is *not* underearning. And if, further, it is something that will also help you to get free of underearning or make that process easier, then it is desirable to do. And since it is in the service of your liberation, it should therefore be a source of self-esteem rather than embarrassment or shame; it took courage and commitment to do it.

The range of resources available to you can be great, depending upon your situation. Some people are qualified for government assistance, such as unemployment benefits, Medicaid, food stamps, housing supplements, aid to dependent children, Social Security payments, and the like. Many corporations have employee assistance programs. There are private agencies, such as Volunteer Lawyers for the Arts. Unions sometimes help with goods, money, and scholarships. Community centers may provide counseling services or a place where children can stay after school. The Legal Aid Society often represents tenants under threat of eviction.

Sharon, a graphic designer with two children, exhausted what little savings she had during her bitterly contested divorce. Her estranged husband, punitive and obsessive, sued for custody of their children. Sharon went more than $30,000 into debt to her lawyer before, as the first major step in freeing herself from underearning, she resolved not to incur any new debt—no matter what she had to do. Briefly, she represented herself in court. But she was frightened by that and didn't do well. Through a friend, she made contact with a shelter for battered women. Though emotionally abused during her marriage, Sharon had never been physically abused. Ordinarily the shelter did not help in such cases, but because of Sharon's persistent entreaties, it finally did refer her to a lawyer. He examined her situation and agreed to represent her pro bono. Thus Sharon was able to get what she needed for herself and her children without incurring any new debt, which was a crucial step in her liberation. Since then, she has been able to raise her income steadily and has even begun, on a small level, to repay her previous debts.

Seeking to learn what help is available, then asking for it (and in some cases becoming willing to accept it) is not easy. But it *is* self-care, it *is* a step forward, and you *are* entitled to it. By availing yourself of it, you assist and strengthen your liberation. You will give back much more than you receive. You will give it back through your recovery. You will give it back to everyone with whom you come into contact. Your recovery will become a part of all that is positive in the world.

What's Right Is Right

Sue the bastard (bitch).

If he ran out on you and stuck you with bills, if she looted your joint bank account, if he or she charged your credit card and store accounts up to the maximum and left you to pay for everything, or dumped the children on you or won't help with their support, then it's time to get tough.

I am in favor of, and to the best of my ability practice, looking upon all beings with eyes of compassion. Nevertheless, and not contradictorily, I am also in favor of requesting, and forcing if necessary and when possible, all beings to honor their financial responsibilities to their former spouses and the children they sired or bore.

This kind of assistance is *owed* to you by your former partner. It's especially important for you to seek it when you are an underearner—and therefore already have a powerful impulse to say no to money. You are *entitled* to help from your former partner. You are entitled to it in an amount that fairly represents your situation and his, or hers.

Maybe your partner has disappeared intentionally and you don't know where he or she is. That happens. But finding someone is usually easier than most people think. The simplest, most effective way to do it is to hire a private investigative agency, preferably one run by ex-law enforcement agents. You can find a reliable one through a friend or an attorney.

When you do know where your former spouse is but he or she refuses to take responsibility, the courts may help. They are becoming increasingly firm in requiring noncustodial parents to pay their fair share of the costs of raising their children. Recently the federal government has indicated that it may become involved in forcing such parents to meet their responsibilities too.

There are no guarantees here. You might not be able to find your former spouse. The court may be unwilling or unable to compel him or her to pay for expenses charged to your joint accounts or to make an equitable contribution toward supporting your children. (Also, you need to weigh your legal costs against the possible benefits; sometimes the equation just isn't in your favor.) But whatever the ultimate results, take what sensible actions you can. What's right is right, and you are not unfair in asking for that principle to be upheld.

IN CLOSING

Hardball and Optimism

Freedom from underearning is not for people who need it. It's for people who want it.

If you're married to or live with someone who is also an underearner but who won't admit that, or who refuses to take any steps toward recovery or even to cooperate with you in your own, not even to the simple extent, say, of drawing up a Household Spending Plan with you, then you're in a difficult situation.

Your best tack is optimism. Just go about your own liberation and assume that in time there will be a resolution that serves your best interests, individually and together. Assume that your own life will grow ever calmer, deeper, and richer because of this, and that sooner or later your partner won't be able to help but notice and eventually to want a similar experience for himself or herself. Don't argue, plead, or cajole. Don't try to proselytize. None of that will work. Simply live your own recovery—for your own sake—in the knowledge that it is the best and most loving thing you can do for your partner.

Sometimes this tack works. Sometimes it doesn't. But regardless of what happens with your partner, this is the best thing you can do for *yourself*.

For a while.

Eventually there will come a time when it is no longer reasonable to assume that continuing in this fashion will result in a positive resolution. That time could be a year. It could be two years, or three. Or it could be a few months. Only you can determine. But when it does arrive—if it does—you have a hard decision to make. If your partner will have nothing to do with getting free of underearning, you have three choices:

One: Stay with him, in the knowledge that he will probably never change. Stay with the understanding that you are *choosing* this situation, that you recognize, comprehend, and accept it for what it is, that you voluntarily elect to remain in it. In this case, you will probably perceive more that is good in the circumstance than bad, deem it livable as it is, and believe you can undertake your own liberation in its context without impossible difficulty.

Two: Try to persuade your partner to change. You might negotiate, for example, trading an activity she would like you to do, or to cease doing, in exchange for her sitting down with you and drawing up a Household Spending Plan together. You could ask her to read this book, to go into counseling with you, or to a support group—even if only to listen and observe. Perhaps she would be willing to talk to a cleric or a friend about the problem. You might write her a long letter, expressing your love and explaining why you think such a change would be good for her and for you both as a couple.

This kind of approach is potentially explosive. So whatever you do, do it lovingly and as free of judgment and criticism as you can. Otherwise, your partner will probably only become angry and resist even more strenuously.

If you exhaust every option you can think of here and there is no change, you can either accept the situation, as described earlier, decide to give it more time, or deliver an ultimatum, a warning that you find the situation intolerable and that unless your partner takes at least some steps toward trying to improve it, you are going to leave or do whatever is necessary to see that she leaves.

Three: Leave, or see that your partner does. This is an extremely serious step. I am not suggesting that you take it. I present it here only as one of the three choices available to you. If you do consider leaving or causing your partner to leave, then do so carefully. Be aware of all the consequences and ramifications of such an act. Write them down so you can see them clearly. Talk to your cleric, therapist, or someone else you trust to be objective and have your best interests at heart. Even in the few situations I've known where it was clearly in the best interest of the recovering underearner to end the relationship, it still, and inescapably, involved a great deal of pain and upheaval.

Hardball is necessary, but optimism about it is always best. It will make things easier for you and for everyone else as well. Further, the very act of expecting a positive outcome will make such an outcome more likely.

Live and Let Live

Finally, live and let live. Live your own life, as you choose, and let your partner, your grown children, and everyone else you know live their lives as they choose—or for reasons beyond your ken, perhaps as they must. Attend to the beam in your own eye; the motes in theirs are their business. It is your birthright to live as you wish, it is theirs to do the same.

Your liberation depends only on you. Theirs, if they are underearners, depends only on them.

It is possible that we *do* know sometimes what is best for another adult. It is also possible that we don't. To assume that we do is arrogance, to try to force that assumption on someone is tyranny.

"Never try to teach a pig to think," goes an old maxim. "It won't work, and will only annoy the pig."

And every missionary looking at a pig, is a pig looking at a missionary.

Therefore, be kind to yourself, and to everyone else: Live, and let live.

PART III
EXPANSION

7.

GROWING STRONGER

THE CONCEPTS AND TECHNIQUES IN THIS CHAPTER ARE PRIMARILY
spiritual. *Spiritual* is a baffling and mysterious word for some;
others are irritated by it. If you have difficulty with it, as I
once did (my early experience of religion having been brutal),
you might find it helpful to look upon this material as essentially psychological. Whatever way you find that allows you to
work with it, please do work with it.

Why?

Because you'll only deprive yourself if you don't. Each of
these concepts and techniques will help you free yourself from
underearning.

As may be apparent already, what we're after in Prospering
is nothing less than a major shift in consciousness—in the
attitudes, beliefs, and ideas you have about yourself and your
relationship to money. This can be the single most important
factor in determining the ease and comfort with which you
liberate yourself from underearning, and the degree to which,
finally, you prosper—the quality of your life as you experience
it.

You can succeed without such a shift. If you use nothing but the practical techniques and strategies in this book, you will still bring your underearning to a halt and improve your situation. But you'll have a harder time of it, you'll deprive yourself of a great deal of emotional and material gain, and you may well get into trouble again later.

Real fixes take place from within, not without. Nothing external—from stardom to a winning lottery ticket—is going to make your "self" any better. The self is an internal image —who you perceive yourself to be, a composite of your thoughts and beliefs. If that self doesn't change, then you will continue to act and feel just as you did before; and in time, regardless of circumstances, you will produce exactly the same results you did before—in this context, a decline into underearning.

Spirituality, connection with what you understand the life force to be, is a powerful agent not only of centering, of peace and serenity, but of effecting internal change as well. It is a tremendous resource, a deep well of strength and comfort.

All the concepts and techniques in Prospering—practical and spiritual—are developmental; they support and enlarge each other. The more you reflect upon them, the deeper the levels of meaning you'll discover in them; the more you practice them, the more effective they will be. And as you integrate them into your consciousness and work with them, a steady flow of new possibilities will become a regular part of your life.

At a minimum, pick the three techniques from this chapter that you find the most appealing—and begin to practice them. (Ideally, you'll practice them all.)

BREATHING IN

Breathing In is a miniature meditation, a way to focus your consciousness, to center and calm yourself. It is an effective means through which to intervene when your thoughts are racing or your emotions crashing about. It is also pleasurable to do for its own sake, at any time.

Here's how:

Close your eyes (or leave them open and unfocused). Breathe in, following your breath with your awareness in through your nostrils and down into your lungs. As you do, say silently to yourself: *Breathing in, I calm my body.* . . . (And do so, gently.) Then breathe out, following your breath back up from your lungs and out through your nostrils. Say silently to yourself: *Breathing out, I smile.* . . . (And do so, putting a small, kind of Mona Lisa half-smile on your mouth.)

Do this three times.

That's all there is to it. Take a moment to try it now. Set the book down. And:

Breathing in, I calm my body. . . . *Breathing out, I smile.* . . .
Breathing in, I calm my body. . . . *Breathing out, I smile.* . . .
Breathing in, I calm my body. . . . *Breathing out, I smile.* . . .

Good. Be aware of how you felt while you did that, and just after. Let yourself enjoy the feeling.

Use this technique whenever you feel yourself growing tense, angry, or fearful—before entering an office for a meeting, for example, or making a difficult telephone call.

Go off by yourself for a minute or two, if you can. If you can't, you can still undertake this exercise nearly anywhere, under nearly any conditions. I sometimes do it walking down the street, or even in a crowded, racketing New York City subway car. Do it on a daily basis for a month. Once you're experienced with it, you may well find that you want to make it a part of your normal everyday life.

NOTICING YOURSELF

In this technique you notice yourself as you would a cup on the table or a tree—without judgment, without analysis, with no attempt to change. You simply observe yourself. It is a practice that will help you grow more comfortable being who you are, regardless of how or what you might have thought of yourself up to now.

Take a moment to try it now.

Become aware of yourself with your consciousness; observe yourself. You may be in a chair or on a couch. Your legs may be crossed, or your feet may be flat against the floor. You are holding this book in some manner or another. You are reading. You are concentrating; or your focus is fragmented. You are breathing. You have an emotion of some kind, perhaps only lightly, as a slight hum in the background. You have energy, or are tired, or maybe neutral. Observe these things and any others you become aware of about yourself—but do not form any opinion about what you observe.

There is no right or wrong in what you see: no failure or success, nothing either desirable or undesirable, to approve of or disapprove of. There is only what you observe—which does not *mean* anything. It just is, and you are observing it: without opinion, emotion. Simply *notice* yourself. Simply *observe* yourself. Simply be *aware* of yourself.

Have you done that? If you have, good. Breathe. Relax. Let yourself shift back into whatever state you were in before you did the exercise. If you haven't done it, consider giving it a try.

There is no point in this exercise beyond itself.

Truly.

Do not try to employ it toward any goal—you'll only be wasting your time.

But paradoxically, if you do practice it—just for the sake of practicing it—change will occur within you. And that change will be to your good, will make it easier for you to free yourself from underearning.

A variation on this technique is simply to notice your emotions, in the same nonjudgmental way, with no purpose beyond observing. If you are feeling anger, simply *notice* that you are feeling anger. Say to yourself, "Ah, I observe that I am feeling anger." If you are feeling joy, simply *notice* that you are feeling joy. Say to yourself, "Ah, I observe that I am feeling joy." Neither applaud nor condemn any emotion, or try to change it. But don't engage with it either. Simply notice that you are feeling it, observe that you are feeling it.

Do this twice a day for a week or two, for a few minutes at a time. Then decide whether you'd like to continue with it.

SEEING

Seeing is way to expand the breadth of your consciousness and bring you more fully into your own life. When we look about, we detect and notice things, register that they are there, but rarely do we *see* them, in the sense of their real presence, their fullest dimensions. Actually, there's a certain usefulness in this, in *not* seeing them; probably no one but true mystics or the most adept among us could cope with such perceptual overload on a regular basis.

But there is a liability in this *not* seeing, too, and that is that most of us never develop the capacity to *see* at all. (Or perhaps the capacity atrophies or is suppressed; it's possible that a form of it exists in young children.) And without *seeing* or at least occasional resort to it, we tend to live on a more limited, superficial, and therefore more painful level.

This technique is meant to develop your ability to *see*. It bears some similarity to Buddhist object meditation. It is simple to practice—here is how:

Stand or sit. Breathe deeply a few times and relax. Look at something, anything at all—a pen, a stone, a laser printer, a fireplace, chair, cup. Without straining, focus your attention on the object. Let your vision play over it. Notice its shape, angles, textures. Begin to *see* it, to take it in. See its parts. Its whole. Mark the shadows on it, its colors. Let its reality enter into your consciousness: its weight, mass, composition; its solidity, complexity. Allow a sense of the object's *existence* to flood into your mind, its presence, its *being*. Do not try to do or think anything about the object; just remain focused on it, open and attentive to it, and let it present itself ever more completely to you.

As with most such practices, the experience of this is difficult to articulate. It is a nonverbal experience, nonrational, a knowing that occurs in a deeper part of the consciousness than the reason can apprehend. What follows is an attempt to suggest a sense of the experience. It is an account by Bob, a medical writer, who meditates only irregularly:

> This happened to me spontaneously. I wasn't meditating, wasn't trying to invoke anything. What was going on was that I'd decided to do a kind of nonwritten gratitude list. I intended just to look around, notice some of the things I was grateful for. This, rather than sit down at my desk and write out a list of them. It wasn't any big thing, just a couple of minutes I was going to spend, a kind of psychological pep-me-up.
>
> I started in a corner of my den, where I work. I figured I'd just look at things, work my way along one wall and maybe part of another. There was a Beardsley print of *John and Salome*—nice, sexy, I like it. A club chair. Leather, stuffed, really good to read in; a good thing in my life. An

art deco cabinet in which I keep some supplies. Pretty. A bookcase, books: comforting, friendly. My answering machine. . . .

I was looking at the answering machine. It's a couple of years old. Workaday, nothing special. It makes my life easier. I recognized that, appreciated the fact, and was about to move on. But I kept looking at the answering machine. I was becoming ever more aware of it, saw its metal case, saw the plastic dial that counts messages, the rocker switch that turns it on and off. . . .

Everything else started to fade. . . . All I saw was the answering machine, and I started to see it all—nicks, screws, dust on the clear plastic strip over the tape, the wire coming out of it. . . . Only there weren't *words* for these things, they weren't *ideas*, I was just *seeing* them. I didn't even know I was doing that, I was just doing it. And I saw the *function* of this thing as a concept, and then suddenly, suddenly it was like an explosion, but not violent, just instantaneous. I saw, or became aware of, or knew somehow, about thousands of people, hundreds of thousands maybe, millions maybe, that were connected to this thing, millennia of history, ore in rocks, metallurgy, mining, the plastic in the thing from oil, billion-year-old vegetation rotting, electronics, thoughts, people working, the creation of all the endless elements and permutations that came into confluence here. . . .

It took my breath away. I felt utterly pure, like crystal, electrified. It was an epiphany. Language collapses, is not adequate to this.

It seemed I was in this state for two or three minutes. But I don't think that's possible. It was probably only three or four seconds—maybe no more than an instant. I don't know.

Anyway, then it was over. I felt weak without feeling

infirm—just a kind of eerie, not unpleasant lightness. I sat down and just sat for a while, breathing, not feeling terribly much of anything. After about ten minutes or so, I got up and went about my day. There was nothing extraordinary about the rest of the day. It was just a very nice one.

It stays with me, that experience. Not as something I can feel but as something I remember that I felt, without being able to feel again. Something like the difference between a photograph of a tree and a tree. Did it apotheosize me somehow, revolutionize my life? No. I am pretty much as I was before . . . but at the same time I'm different. I find it hard to determine how. For one thing, I don't think I've ever been truly as afraid as I sometimes was before, though I certainly have known fear since then. I don't know. It's different. Better or worse aren't applicable words. It's just different. And I'm glad of it.

Seeing is probably not something most of us can or will do on a daily basis. And it's not something we can mine for results or from which we can even expect anything. It is nearly always different in its particularities, while—on some elemental level—nearly always similar. Engage in it, if you choose to, with whatever frequency or infrequency you wish. People who do it are, in Bob's words, generally glad of it.

CASTING OUT DEVILS (IN A MANNER OF SPEAKING)

This is a way to help you change negative emotions about your work and your money for the better. It will also increase the likelihood of your actions bringing favorable results.

It's important to know that your emotions are simply that —emotions. They are not facts. They are not evidence of the way things really are. They are, in fact, little more than reflections of your own thoughts and perceptions. You may, for example, feel that your problems are overwhelming and hopeless, but that doesn't mean that they *are* overwhelming and hopeless.

This is an important distinction. It is appropriate to feel fear if a large, savage dog lunges through an open gate at you; or grief at the death of a loved one. But most fear and despondency stem primarily from your cognitions, from what you *think*. Ancient sailors experienced fear when storms blew their ship far out to sea. They became afraid they would fall off the edge of the earth. Despite the intensity of their fear, which was generated entirely by what they *thought* might happen, they were not going to fall off the edge. Their emotions were simply that—emotions. They did not reflect the actual facts.

Most of your negative emotions are the result of fatalistic and gloomy scenarios that play in your mind, of what you *imagine*.

The Book of Proverbs says, "For as [a man] thinketh in his heart, so is he."

Henry Ford said, "If a man tells you he can or cannot do a job, he's right."

The *Dhammapada*, one of Buddhism's favorite texts, begins: "All we are is the result of what we have thought."

Clinical research has demonstrated that the human central nervous system cannot distinguish between a vividly imagined event and an actual event; it responds the same way to both. In practical terms, this means that my emotional response to *thinking* that a story will probably be rejected, to imagining that, will be close to the response I would have if the story actually *were* rejected. The major part of what we feel is determined by what we *think*. And whenever I think in negative scenarios, I experience emotions appropriate to real events.

The further problem with imagined negative scenarios is

that the very act of imagining them can actually bring them about. If I had thought, for example, "There's no point in writing a book about underearning—no one will ever buy it," then I wouldn't have written this book. And since I wouldn't have written it, no one would have bought it.

My thought would have created my reality.

In picturing an event, I am actually *rehearsing* myself to experience it. Preparing to dive, an Olympic diver does not picture herself losing stride as she nears the end of the board, half slipping instead of springing from it, twisting and flailing awkwardly in the air as she attempts to right herself, and slamming into the water on her belly. Just the opposite. Yet that is precisely what we do, and how we rehearse ourselves, when we run through a negative event in our head.

When Ian, a photographer, first began to work with the Casting Out Devils technique, he was startled by the sheer number of negative statements, judgments, scenes, and projections he found looming up in his mind. So startled that he went to a sporting goods store and bought a wrist-counter, the kind golfers use to record their strokes. The next day, he pressed the button each time a negative thought entered his mind, anything from "He's a bastard" to seeing himself losing his major account. He counted 137 such thoughts by the time the day was over. Neither Ian, nor you, nor I can even hope to get through a day with equanimity bombarded by that much negativity.

So what can we do about this? First, do not try to repress or crush the negative thought by brute force of will. That's not very effective. Instead, recognize and acknowledge that it's there—without blaming yourself or being disappointed with yourself for having it.

Then, say silently to yourself: "I reject and dissolve this scenario. It is not for my highest good or the highest good of anyone else involved."

Next, replace the negative thought or scenario with a new one, one that *does* represent the highest good for you and everyone else involved.

Charlotte, a painter who worked part time as a data processor, experienced agony each time she made an appointment for a prospective client to view her artwork. It would look as if she were begging for money, she felt. The client would be contemptuous of her work, think she was incompetent, reject her. She knew she would be humiliated and unable to paint for days. There would be no money. She would have to give up painting altogether and take a full-time job.

All this went on in Charlotte's *head*—yet her emotions, in response to her thoughts, were as searingly painful as if such events had actually happened. Further, as a natural result, she found it difficult to make appointments with possible clients. Sometimes she even broke one she'd already made. As a direct consequence, she sold fewer paintings than she would have otherwise, which meant there was indeed less money in her life, which in turn made the possibility of her having to take a full-time job far more likely.

Here is how Charlotte worked with Casting Out Devils once she began to use it:

As soon as she realized she was playing out a negative script in her mind, she acknowledged that to herself, without judgment.

Then she said silently: "I reject and dissolve this scenario. It is not for my highest good or the highest good of anyone else involved."

(Which was certainly true.)

Next, she pictured the client coming to her studio, enjoying this glimpse into the artist's life, taking pleasure in his conversation with her, looking through her canvases with knowledgeable appreciation, being torn between two of them, then making a decision, writing her out a check, thanking her, and saying he knew another collector he was sure would want to see her work and asking if she would mind him giving that person her number.

Did casting out negative scenarios and replacing them with ones that served everyone's highest good radically alter Charlotte's career and catapult her to the top of the New York art scene? No, it did not. But what it did do was eliminate most of Charlotte's painful emotions around inviting clients to her studio and replace them with pleasurable ones. That made it easier for her to make such appointments, which increased the number of prospective buyers who did see her work, which in turn led to her selling more of her paintings than she had before.

Wonderful. But what happened when a client came and didn't buy, perhaps even (God forbid!) actually *did* think she was incompetent? In those cases Charlotte had to deal with her disappointment and self-judgment. But at least she did not inflict that disappointment upon herself beforehand by imagining such a scene; nor, more important, did she deprive herself of sales by avoiding appointments because of her fearful imaginings.

As you work the various parts of Prospering, your thoughts will evolve into more positive and beneficial ones. But that will take a while—you've probably been experiencing negative scenarios for a long time and in great numbers, which isn't something you can reverse overnight. In the meantime, use Casting Out Devils (in a Manner of Speaking) to intervene in the negative process directly, right now, when it needs to be intervened in. This is neither denial nor repression; it is simply taking active control of your own thought process, which is a learned skill.

This technique may seem awkward at first, and perhaps even difficult, but you'll find it easier and more natural to practice as you gain experience. In time, it may become nearly a reflex.

BECOMING FREE

Resentment has been called the root of all spiritual disease, and it may be. Certainly it is toxic: physically, emotionally, psychologically, and spiritually. Resentment can generate, for example, gastritis (a physical problem), rage (emotional), obsession (psychological), and disconnection (spiritual).

Resentment is lethal to underearners. It dominates their consciousness, consumes their energy, blinds them to possibilities, and can cause them to deprive themselves out of a desire to punish someone ("Look how badly you hurt me— you crippled me, made me incapable and miserable!") or, less frequently, guilt over having the resentment.

Resentment is not the same thing as anger.

Anger is a temporary flare of hostility or wrath. A speeding cab swerves around traffic, hits a puddle, and sprays you with dirty water. You feel a surge of hostility, raise your fist, spit out an obscenity. But a few minutes later, you're breathing normally again, you've stopped muttering to yourself, and you're thinking in practical terms about how to deal with your soiled pants for the rest of the afternoon. The heat, the severe emotion, is gone.

Not so with resentment.

Resentment is an *abiding* anger. A *bitter* anger. It is hatred. Blame. A burning sense of grievance. A hunger for retribution. The word comes from the Latin prefix *re-* ("again") and the verb *sentir* ("to feel"). Literally, *resentment* means "to feel again." And again, and again. Over and over, endlessly.

Marge, a severe underearner through most of her adult life, now in her sixties, was speaking bitterly about a painful injustice she had suffered at the hands of her older sister when she was fourteen. Her listener had already heard this tale several times. "Marge," he said, "that was *half a century* ago—and your sister's been *dead* for twenty years."

"Yes!" Marge said, her mouth twisted in fury. "And I'll *never* forget!"

Sadly, she probably never will.

Resentment, for anyone, is a costly luxury—it steals away delight, peace, joy; it makes comfort unavailable, love impossible. For underearners, it is deadly.

If any single factor in itself can make liberation from underearning impossible, it is resentment.

The bile, acid, spite, virulence, shrieking fury, and agony of resentment wreak most of their damage not upon the person who is resented but upon the one who holds the resentment. Resentment is a form of self-destruction. With underearners, this destruction nearly always manifests itself in continued and even worsening underearning. Any resentment you feel needs to be gotten free of—for your own sake.

The most effective way to free yourself of resentment is through forgiveness, by forgiving whomever you feel resentful toward. Actually, forgiveness will never fail to free you.

"But how can I possibly forgive *him!*"

"After what she *did* to me?"

Forgiveness is an alien concept to some people, particularly those whose resentments are deep and intense or who have been clinging to them for years. It is important to know this. The point of forgiving is not to earn Heaven points or to become virtuous but *to free yourself from pain*—to help *you* liberate *yourself* from underearning. It's also important to know that to forgive does not mean to condone or to excuse behavior. You may indeed have been treated shamefully, even hideously. But that is not the point. The point is for *you* to become free of the resentment, so that *you* can live a better, happier, and more prosperous life.

Here is a powerful way to achieve forgiveness. In bed, just

before sleep, relax. Quiet your mind. Breathe easily. Become still. Then, using the first name of whomever you feel resentful toward, say silently to yourself, and with as much sincerity and genuineness as you can muster:

"[Name], I fully and freely forgive you. I completely loose you and let you go. I do not wish to hurt you. I wish you no harm. So far as I am concerned, this incident [trouble] between us is over forever. You are free, and I am free, and all is well again between us."

Even the *thought* of saying such a thing makes some people gag—which only indicates how powerful and deeply entrenched the resentment is. The final phrase—"and all is well again between us"—does not mean that you need to embrace this person or welcome him back into your life. It might mean that, it might not. It may mean that you never see or deal with him again. But what it definitely *does* mean is that you will be at peace over the issue, and that a blocked channel will have been opened, through which more life, including freer earning, can now flow.

For many people, this technique—which is at once a prayer, a meditation, an affirmation, and a declaration to one-self—is very difficult at first. If that is your experience, don't fret about it. Just summon up however much sincerity you can as you say the words, even if that isn't much at all. You'll find that more will come as you proceed, until finally you will be able to forgive the person completely. Sometimes the experience of that—of total forgiveness—lasts only an instant, is experienced as a kind of epiphany.

Work with a single resentment at a time. Stay with it until you feel the forgiveness is complete. If a particular resentment proves resistant, alternate periods of working on it with periods of setting it aside for a while. Many people find they can realize forgiveness—and through that, release—by practicing this exercise with a given resentment each night for a week or so. Occasionally someone discovers she accomplishes forgiveness almost instantly. Other resentments require more time.

Here is another effective technique:

Relax and quiet yourself. Then picture the face of the person toward whom you are resentful. Now, mentally, give to him all of the same things you would like to have yourself: money, a beautiful house, peace, health, a wonderful job, children, fame—anything you would like for yourself, *everything* you would like for yourself.

Christine, a comedienne, literally shook with refusal and rage when this was suggested to her. She bitterly resented another performer who she felt had cheated her out of an apartment a few years earlier and who, she further believed, had cost her a television role by deprecating her to the producer.

"No!" she said. "Never, never! I *hate* her. I want her dead!"

And in this, Christine was telling the truth. She did hate the woman, did want her dead. Nevertheless, though wildly resistant, she forced herself to try the technique: Christine was a lifelong underearner who was willing to go to any lengths to stop underearning. The best she could manage on her first attempt was a few seconds in which she was able to give to the other woman only one thing she wanted for herself—a new pair of running shoes. Then almost instantly her sense of grievance and her fury erupted. She had to stop; was unable to get to sleep for more than an hour. But she tried again the next night, and the next. And in time she was able—fully, freely, and with a sense of goodwill—to give to that woman everything she wanted for herself, including her two most cherished desires: a loving relationship and stardom.

It is now a year later. Christine thinks it is possible that she unknowingly exaggerated the magnitude of the other woman's offense or even misinterpreted what took place. Perhaps she did, perhaps she didn't. Whichever, she is free of a resentment that had tormented her for years—and while it is rarely possible to establish a direct correlation in such matters and while Christine has worked many of the other parts of Prospering, too, the fact remains that her income this past year was more than twice what it was the previous year.

Use these procedures to forgive all the offenses you have ever suffered—real or perceived. Some never *did* take place but were only a matter of our interpretation. Often there is what *I* think happened, what *you* think happened, and what *really* happened.

Begin with resentments that center on money or work, such as alimony you have to pay, or being passed over for a promotion or cheated by a business partner. Later, you can go on to others. (*All* resentments are obstacles to a prosperous life.)

HAVING TEA WITH YOUR EMOTIONS

Once you've had a chance to work with Casting Out Devils and other elements of Prospering, and are able to exercise some choice over your emotions, you're ready to invite your emotions—even the negative ones, even the *horrifying* ones—to sit down and visit with you for a while, to, metaphorically, have a little tea with you.

The primary value of doing this is in discovering that your emotions—no matter what they are—are neither overwhelming nor obliterating, that they do not have the power to annihilate you or render you helpless. You'll discover, in fact, that you can coexist fairly peacefully with even the worst of them.

Let's say that the emotion you're wary of is fear or self-loathing. Don't try to repress it (your old instinct). Or to intervene in it by breathing in and breathing out (one of your new skills). Or even to reject and dissolve the negative scenario that caused it and replace that with a new one (another new skill). Instead, invite the emotion to tea. Sit down with it. Relax. Lower all your defenses. Allow yourself to experience the emotion purely, completely, without resistance. *Be* the emotion: *Be* fear. *Be* self-loathing. Feel it completely. Be within it; let it be within you. Experience it totally.

Do this for as long as five minutes, if you can.

Most people discover that they can't experience an emotion—purely, uninterruptedly—for more than one or two minutes, often for no more than thirty seconds. Not because the emotion is so awesomely powerful that they can't endure it any longer, but because it cannot exist in a pure state much longer than that. It burns itself out, collapses in upon itself, or crests, subsides, and disappears.

Don't try to sustain the emotion beyond what seems its natural life span. Let it burn out or subside when it will. When it passes, when it ceases to be the *totality* of your experience (though there might still be traces left), examine other areas of your self-awareness. Be aware of your senses—what you see, hear, smell, the taste of your own mouth, of what you feel with your body. Be aware of other emotions you have— relief perhaps, exhilaration, or anything else. Be aware of your thoughts, anything from intellectual observation to bits of dialogue, images of things you want to pick up from the store later, half-sensible chatter.

What you learn when you sit down and have tea with an emotion is that emotions you have feared for so long, that have terrified you, that have played a strong role in your underearning, are in reality not monsters at all but only windmills—paper tigers, bogeymen. What has hurt you has not been the emotions themselves but your struggle to resist them, to escape them, or block them out.

It's best to practice this exercise only in the context of the rest of Prospering, which provides an integrated system of support. Otherwise, you're likely to abandon the attempt almost immediately. Even less desirable, you may simply experience the pain without comprehending that it has no real power over you. Moreover, you'll lack the perspective that will allow you to evaluate the experience usefully and become stronger for it, and the techniques through which to ease yourself back into your normal state.

Delay inviting your emotions to sit down to tea until you feel comfortably grounded in Prospering as a whole. After the first few times you do the exercise, you may wish to clear away any of the emotion that lingers on. Use the breathing-in, breathing-out technique at intervals over the ensuing hour; or identify whatever negative scenario is going through your mind, reject and dissolve it, and replace it with a positive one. Another clearing technique is to sit quietly, breathe in and out a few times, then picture—as vividly as you can, using your senses—a scene or event from your past in which you were truly happy: a moment from your childhood, a day of triumph or celebration, a quiet evening by a pond. Be there again, as fully as you can, as *feeling* as you can, without straining, for three or four minutes. Then smile, take a deep breath in and out, stretch, relax, and return to your normal day.

Once you've begun, invite your emotions to tea two or three times a week. After a few months, you'll find yourself doing the exercise less and less often as your emotions assume ever more appropriate, less threatening, proportions in your life. At that point, practice the technique with whatever frequency seems useful to you.

QUIET

Meditation is a vast subject about which innumerable books have been written. It is at once both a simple process and a subtle and complex one. The most important points to make about it, for our purposes, are: First, anyone can meditate, and second, meditation brings many benefits.

Meditation, which comes in a variety of forms, is a mental discipline that enables you to become still, to become utterly quiet in mind and body. It is a quieting of the noise of the world, the ceaseless chatter of one's own mind or a detachment from that noise and chatter. It is a movement inward, toward unity, toward integration with the creative principle of the universe, with pure energy, awareness, and joy. Meditation is an ancient, time-honored practice. Generally, it is associated with the East. But Western religions, while not having emphasized it to the same degree as Eastern religions, also have their own tradition of meditation. In Christianity, it is called contemplative prayer; in Judaism, *kavvanah*.

"Be still," we are told, "and know that I am God."

And: "Thou wilt keep him in perfect peace whose mind is stayed on Thee."

Over the past several decades, Western medical researchers have repeatedly documented meditation's many physical, psychological, intellectual, and emotional benefits. Meditation techniques and practices, if you are unfamiliar with them, can be learned at yoga centers, Buddhist organizations, some Christian retreats, and alternative education centers; in stress-management courses offered by hospitals; and even through books and videotapes. Practically any of meditation's many forms will do. Pick one that feels right for you. Even meditating only once a day, for only ten minutes, will be helpful in the process of freeing yourself from underearning.

In the quiet there is grace and healing.

PRAYER

Prayer, like meditation, has also been recognized for centuries for the support, strength, and comfort it lends to those who undertake it. And prayer, like spirituality, is a personal subject that is often difficult to discuss on anything but an abstract level. Nevertheless, here are some personal comments on how I came to it, for whatever value they may have for you.

It was the early 1980s. I had not prayed in years—decades, actually. I had been strenuously an atheist all my adult life. But I could not help but notice, in this new life without chemicals and without debt that I had begun to lead, that nearly everyone around me who had anything that I wanted in my own life—serenity, delight, joy, the capacity to wake up in the morning with enthusiasm rather than despair—had some kind of connection with some kind of higher power. However they defined that.

So pragmatically, if for no other reason—it seemed to *work*—I wanted to say a prayer. But my early experience with religion had been so murderous and my consequent rejection of that religion so powerful that I could not bring myself to say any prayer I had ever heard in my childhood—indeed, any kind of prayer from any religion. They all rang false, wrong. And I wanted to say a genuine prayer, one I could truly mean. Genuinely, to pray.

But I could find no authenticity within myself with any prayer I knew or had ever encountered. So, over two or three days, I wrote one myself, one I could say without recoiling in disgust, incredulity, or anger, one I could say with all my heart and being, from the deepest recess of myself, one that I could *mean*. The following night, as I lay in bed getting ready for sleep, I relaxed myself, emptied my mind as best I could, and then—with all the genuineness and integrity I could find in myself—I said that prayer, which was this:

"In the unlikely event there is any motivating force in the universe, in the improbability that it is even remotely aware that the species exists, and in the near impossibility that it has in any way contributed to anything that is good in my life—I am appreciative."

I could say that prayer. I could mean it with all my heart. And I did.

It was a beginning.

Prayer is a powerful instrument. It requires no specific form or creed. Anything addressed as a prayer, to any form of higher power, *is* a prayer and offers much. "The function of prayer," wrote the philosopher Kierkegaard, "is not to influence God, but rather to change the nature of the one who prays."

WHO AM I?

This is a specific meditation that can help you achieve balance and proportion while freeing yourself from underearning. It can help you see the many aspects of your life and "self" in tranquil perspective. It is optional. You won't hurt yourself by not doing it. Nor will you fail in any way if you try but seem unable to engage with it.

If you do choose to work with it, it's best to wait until you are experienced with other, more basic forms of meditation, such as breath counting, sensory awareness, or mantra repetition, and have worked some of the earlier techniques in this chapter before you undertake it. When you do begin, practice it lightly at first, for only three or four minutes. Since doing this exercise may challenge an identity that you have long believed in, particularly if focused on too intently or sustained too long by a novice, it can cause psychological or emotional discomfort. Should that occur, simply discontinue the meditation. But if you approach it bearing these admonitions in mind, you will probably have only a positive and beneficial experience with it.

To do it, sit in a chair. Keep your back straight but not stiff. Rest your hands on your thighs, palms facing upward. Close your eyes. Become comfortable, and breathe easily. Relax your body. Let your mind become quiet. Then, as best you can, place your consciousness deep within your diaphragm, in the calm and quiet center of your being.

Now ask yourself silently, "Who am I?"

Maybe, as your first answer, your name comes to mind: *Jerry.*

Say to yourself, easily, without strain:

"No, that is a name people call me. That is not me. Who is the 'I' who is called by that name?"

Perhaps your occupation occurs to you next: *A writer.*

Say to yourself easily, without strain:

"No, writing is something I do. That is not me. Who is the 'I' who does the writing?"

My thoughts.

"No, those are a function of my consciousness. They are not me. Who is the 'I' who has these thoughts?"

My consciousness.

"No, that is something I possess. That is not me. Who is the 'I' who has this consciousness?"

A man.

"No, that is the sex of my body. That is not me. Who is the 'I' who has this sex?"

My body.

Easily, without strain:

"No, that is something I inhabit. That is not me. Who is the I that inhabits this body?"

Fear.

"No, that is an emotion I feel. That is not me. Who is the 'I' who feels this emotion?"

My books.

"No, those are things I created. They are not me. Who is the 'I' who created the books."

A father.

"No, that is a relationship I have. That is not me. Who is the 'I' who has this relationship?"

Ishkabible.

"No, that is a meaningless word that occurred to me. That is not me. Who is the 'I' to whom this word occurred?"

Me.

"No, that is a way I perceive myself. That is not me. Who is the 'I' who perceives itself?"

Rage.

"No, that is an emotion I feel. That is not me. Who is the 'I' who feels this emotion?"

Peace.

"No, that is an emotion I feel. That is not me. Who is the 'I' who feels this emotion?"

Bliss.

"No, that is an emotion I feel. That is not me. Who is the 'I' who feels this emotion?"

God.

"No, that is a concept I have. That is not me. Who is the 'I' who has this concept?"

History.

"No, that is a branch of study I know of. That is not me. Who is the 'I' who knows of this branch of study?"

Inquiry.

Easily, without strain:

"No, that is questioning I do. That is not me. Who is the 'I' who does this questioning . . . ?"

That's what the process looks like. As you do it, don't simply free-associate from one answer to the next. Instead, actively—but without urgency—look for an answer. (Some free association is natural.) Respond to each answer as in the example above. It's important that the responses be structured, to keep the meditation from collapsing. It is equally important that this meditation be easy and without strain. It may be unsettling at times, but it should not be harsh or frightening. If a sense of completion should come over you at any moment while you are in the process, rest in that sense for several moments, then end the meditation.

Here, as in nearly all work of a spiritual nature, trust your own intuition as to how best to proceed—not your intellect, ego, or emotions, but your intuition. As you grow more experienced with spiritual practice, it will be easier to distinguish what is truly your intuition from what is not.

THE HIGHEST THOUGHT

When you are about to engage in any situation that involves both another human being and the flow of money in and through your life—a job interview, negotiation with a client, deal with a creditor—get quiet for a few moments first and think the Highest Thought you can about that person.

What is the Highest Thought? The one that is the:

- Most positive
- Least restricting
- Most loving
  and that . . .
- Feels the best

Thinking the Highest Thought is not to deny or ignore any adversarial or threatening elements that may be present. Rather, it is to refuse to be overcome by them: It is to alter the situation by reframing your perceptions of it, to reposition yourself into clarity, calmness, and greater awareness. With experience, you may find yourself executing this almost automatically, that your dealings with people go more smoothly and pleasurably because of it, and that the results of these dealings are more favorable than they used to be.

MAKING FRIENDS WITH MONEY

Underearners generally do not look upon money as a friend: It never writes, it never calls, it's always hanging out with someone else.

Money has life, and like other living things—like you, like me—it doesn't go where it isn't liked, isn't wanted. It doesn't go where it is feared, lusted after, envied, grabbed at, hoarded, resented, and otherwise made to feel unwelcome.*

So begin treating money well. Don't jam it into your pocket or push it into the bottom of your purse. Put it in your wallet, nicely and neatly. Say hello to it. Tell it how pleased you are to see it, how happy you are it's come to visit. Treat it like a valued guest. And when the time comes for it to move on—as all guests must, and should—bid it farewell and a wonderful journey, happy that it came to visit you and looking forward to your next visitor. Be hospitable. Be a kind, loving, and generous host, into and out of whose life a steady stream of guests are delighted to flow.

Think of every way you can in which to make money feel always welcomed and appreciated in your life. Then treat it in those ways. And when you spend money, say silently to yourself whenever you hand over the cash, or send a check out to

---

* Deal with this as metaphor if you wish—it may be.

someone: "I bless this money. I give it to you. I wish you pleasure in using it."

Make friends with money.

THE SOURCE OF IT

Close your eyes for a moment. Think of the source of your money. Think of where your money comes from.

Do this now, before you read any further. Set the book aside, close your eyes, and think of where your money comes from—all the sources.

Go ahead.

Finished? Good.

Most people think first of their job as the source of their money. Then of additional work they perform, such as consulting, free-lance carpentry, or the like. Then of dividends and interest. And pensions, bonuses, rent from property they own, commissions, Social Security payments, unemployment checks, scholarships, clients, patients, even gifts or help they receive from their families.

Yet none of these, and probably nothing else you pictured, is really the source of your money. The company you work for is not the source of your money, even though it writes your paycheck. Your clients are not the source, even though they pay you. The stocks and bonds you own are not the source. Nor is the government, your friends, your family, or your customers.

Just as the telephone is not the source of your phone calls, nor the mail carrier the source of your letters, but rather the agencies through which those arrive.

The real source of your money is God, or the Universe—or, for the determinedly secular, your Self.

My agent is not the source of my money. Nor is my publisher. Nor anyone who buys my books. The real source of my money—the ultimate source, that from which it truly comes—is God. Or, if you prefer, is me.

The real source of a cabinetmaker's money is not his client, but his skill with his hands, his feel for wood, knowledge of grain, eye for space, sense of design and aesthetics. *He* is the source of his money, not any other person or company or organization or government.

The source of a basketball player's money is not the team that pays him, but he *himself*, his height, his eye-hand coordination, his willingness to practice long hours, his ability to cooperate with his teammates.

And *you* are the source of your money, not the company that pays you.

This is good news: It means that you need never really fear the loss of your job, a fall in real estate values, a shift in the market or economy, or the alteration of any other outside person, place, or thing. Because none of those is the real source of your money. They are simply agencies through which your money arrives. And agencies change. When one closes down, as they will, the source remains unaltered. It is necessary to know that the source remains unchanged and constant. Difficulty occurs only when the channel, or agency, is mistaken for the source.

How does one go about truly coming to understand that and be comfortable in it? By returning repeatedly to the concept intellectually and by using the analogies given in this topic to help grasp it—while working the other parts of Prospering.

AN ANONYMOUS ACT OF GENEROSITY

Some underearners hang on to every dime as if it were the last morsel of food on earth, spending only under duress or when absolutely necessary. This is a miserable way to live. Worse, it blocks the flow of new money into your life. Money is not static. It needs open channels through which to flow. When you congest it this way, when all your energies and focus are given over to defending what you have, you simply reinforce your belief that there is not enough for you, and prevent more of it from coming in.

Here is a practice that will help you demolish that belief in lack and scarcity and connect you with the easy, free, and natural flow of money through your life. It will calm you and engage you more actively with that flow. This is how you do it:

Place the residential pages of your telephone directory on your desk. Close your eyes. Open the directory at random and put your finger somewhere on the page. Open your eyes. Write down the name and address your finger has fallen on. (Most directories include a map with zip code information; if yours doesn't, call the post office to get the zip code.)

Now pick an amount of money. Make it an amount somewhere between one you could toss off easily, like a dollar or two, and one whose loss you would truly feel. For many people that may be $20, $30, or $50; for others it might be $5, or $100. Whatever it is, decide on a figure.

Now place that amount in cash, along with an anonymous note (which we'll discuss below), inside an envelope. Seal the envelope. Address it to the person you randomly selected from the phone book, put a stamp on the envelope, and mail it.

Give the money away.

To a stranger.

For the sheer sake of giving, of sharing.

The purpose of the note is to explain what you are doing, so you don't unsettle or alarm the person who receives the money. He or she may be a little uneasy at first, but that will pass pretty quickly, especially if your note is clear. You might want to write something like this:

Dear [Name]:

I don't know you. You don't know me. I picked your name at random out of the telephone book, and will have no record of it, will not keep it in memory after I mail this.

Money comes into my life, and I am grateful for that. I'm expressing my appreciation for it to the Universe by passing money along, by sharing what I have received.

Bless you. May you know peace, joy.

However you phrase your note, be sure to include some form of explanation and assurance. Type the note if you can, which helps keep it impersonal, but sign it in longhand, which adds a measure of the personal. *Do not sign it with your name.* That would destroy the anonymity and deprive you of the value of this act. You are not seeking acknowledgment or thanks here—you are giving for the sheer sake of giving. You might want to sign the note "A Fellow Human Being," "A Fellow Traveler on the Planet," "Just Someone Else in Life," or something similar. For the return address, repeat the name and address of the recipient.

When you drop the envelope into the mailbox, simply smile, bless the person who will receive this money, bless the universe from which you received it, and then forget about it. Do not save the recipient's name anywhere. Let the name slip from your mind and be gone. Do not fantasize about how he or she might react, or on what the money might be spent. Be done with it. Your only involvement is in the act of giving and in blessing this person when you mail the letter.

Some people find the prospect of this exhilarating; others are appalled by it. Judy, a woman who works in the employee assistance program of her company, refused even to consider the possibility when it was suggested at a workshop. She found the idea of giving money to someone she didn't know, and who would never know it was she who had given it, incomprehensible and infuriating. Bill, a young account assistant at the same workshop, was so delighted by it that he broke into spontaneous grins through the rest of the day and planned to execute it as soon as he got home that night.

Giving money, for an underearner, is much more impactful than giving time, services, or personally made gifts. Giving money, when you give, makes money more real to you, heightens your awareness of it, and increases your confidence in your ability to generate it.

Why, if you are giving, do so anonymously—and to a stranger? Giving to your church, an environmental fund, a medical cause, or any other program you support is perfectly fine and a good thing to do. But an anonymous act of generosity, giving to another human being about whom you know nothing at all except that he or she shares life with you, with whom you will have contact only for this instant, without an agenda of any kind, puts you most completely and most purely in contact with the unadulterated act of giving.

Which will resound deeply within you, and likely in remarkable and unforeseen ways.

Do this as often as you wish.

GOOD LUCK, BAD LUCK

Here, as we draw near the end of this chapter, is a topic that is more concept than technique, but that, like contemplating the source of your money, gains the practical value of a technique when brought to mind often. It is in the form of a very old tale, a Taoist tale. I will provide it as it has been handed down:

An old farmer had but a single horse. One day the horse ran off into the mountains. To plow the fields, the old man and his son had to put the traces around their own shoulders.

When neighbors heard of the event, they came and sympathized saying, "Oh, your horse ran off. What bad luck!"

The farmer sighed. "Bad luck, good luck—who knows?"

The following week, the horse returned to the farm, bringing with it a large herd of wild horses from the mountains.

Hearing of this, the neighbors came to congratulate the old farmer. "You are a wealthy man with this herd! What good luck!"

The old man shrugged. "Good luck, bad luck—who knows?"

The next week, while trying to break one of the wild horses to saddle, the old man's son was thrown from it and his leg was broken.

The neighbors came to commiserate with the farmer. "It will be months before he can get out of bed. What bad luck!"

The old man said, "Bad luck, good luck—who knows?"

The week after that, the ruler's army swept through the

valley, forcing all the young men to go off with it to fight the enemy. Seeing that the farmer's son could not walk, they left him where he was.

The neighbors came to celebrate with the old man. "The army did not take your son away to fight," they said. "What good luck!"

After a moment, the farmer said, "Good luck, bad luck —who knows?"

TRANSFORMING THE WORLD

No, this isn't a vision of deliverance, as the name might indicate. It's just a quiet little practice.

How is the world changed? By bayonets, by wealth, by technology. By and through a host of ways, many violent, none lasting. Civilizations rise and fall. Philosophies replace each other. Regimes come and go.

Change is simply that—change.

But transformation is something entirely different.

Would you transform the world? Then perform small acts of kindness. That is the only way it will ever be transformed, altered in a fundamental way. It makes no difference under whose banner you are shot, or shoot someone else. If the world can be transformed, be made a better place to live, then that will be done little by little, like a trickle of water eventually scratching out a great canyon.

You will never live to see the world become as you would like it to be. Nor will I. But you will live to see it transformed. You will see it be transformed—become something better than what it was—each time you perform a small act of kindness, even if that is nothing but to smile at someone on the street.

And what if the world is not transformed by such an act?

Well, then it isn't. But what definitely will be, to no matter how small a degree, is your own life. *That* will become a better place for you to live, which is a part of prospering.

AND FINALLY . . .

Establish in your home some object, center, or place of peace. Something that represents or invites the stillness. Something that helps you to become still and turn your focus inward, toward the animating principle, the elemental life force, whatever you may perceive it to be.

This can be a statue, a prayer bell, a mandala, a visage, an arrangement of stones or flowers. It can be a chair in which you meditate, with a plant beside it. It can be a brass bowl in which you burn incense, or a piece of wood or pottery. It can be an aquarium with fish moving slowly through the water, in front of which you can sit and become quiet, contemplative, peaceful.

Make such a place in your home soon. And make such a place in your heart.

You have covered a great deal of ground in this chapter and acquainted yourself with powerful vehicles of change. You may want to close the book now and put it away for the night, to continue your reading tomorrow. If you do, consider meditating for a while after you set the book down, then perhaps going for a walk or doing something else that is easy and pleasurable for the next ten or fifteen minutes. If it is late, perhaps you might simply sit quietly for a few minutes, smiling if you wish, before turning off the light and going to sleep.

PART IV
THE STEPS

8.

STEPS ONE THROUGH SIX

THIS FINAL SECTION OF THE BOOK DEALS WITH THE TWELVE Steps—a set of spiritual principles (or actions) that originated in Alcoholics Anonymous—and ways to work with them to help free yourself from underearning. Together the Steps describe the actions taken by the early members of AA in their successful quest to get sober and stay sober. We'll discuss the first six in this chapter, and the other six in Chapter 9.

Working with the Steps is not to everyone's taste, particularly at first. But great numbers of people—not just alcoholics—have used them to powerful effect to help free themselves from problematic and self-destructive behaviors around food, relationships, and most significant for our purposes, money.

Don't allow yourself to be intimidated or put off by the severity of the problems that some people who have worked the Steps have had, or dismiss their value to you because of that. They are potent tools for anyone who wants to liberate himself or herself from underearning.

The Steps are not presented in AA or any of the other Anonymous programs as something people *must* do in order to succeed with whatever difficulty they're addressing. Rather, they are presented as suggestions, actions to take that will facilitate and strengthen recovery.

I offer them here in the same spirit. (And truly hope you'll take me up on the suggestion.) You have nothing to lose and potentially a great deal to gain by working with them, particularly if you think you might be a chronic, habitual, or even compulsive underearner. You can only deepen and make more abiding your recovery.

Also, you'll find that in a way you've already begun. Techniques such as Mirror, Mirror, on the Wall, Noticing Yourself, and Becoming Free, accomplish work at the same levels and in some of the same areas addressed by the Steps.

Step work can be deeply personal. Because of that, I have relied more on my own life in this part of the book for examples than I have in others, and am particularly grateful to those people who were generously willing to share some of *their* experiences here.

Nary a Sect, Denomination, or Religion in Sight

Much has been written about the Steps (though nothing from the perspective of underearning), and doubtless much more will be. I wish to make only two observations about them in this section.

First, despite occasional theorizing to the contrary, the Steps are not drawn from any sect or denomination, or indeed even from any particular religion. It is true, as some people have pointed out, that the Steps were formulated in the Christian climate of early twentieth-century America, and that something resembling a couple of them had been part of the Oxford Group, a religious reform movement that had flourished a little earlier and whose concepts were of some influence on AA in its first years. But it is also true that *all* of the Steps, in one form or another, can be found in Marcus Aurelius's *Meditations*, written nearly twenty centuries ago and unrelated to Christianity, and that the essence of the Steps appears in the work of philosophers like Heraclitus and Epictetus, can be found in Taoist tales and the poems of Chuang Tzu, heard in the Psalms and Book of Proverbs, and read in the Upanishads and Vedas. Indeed, the substance of the Steps echoes in some fashion through nearly all the sacred writings of the world.

Second, what is unique about the Steps *as* the Steps is the particular combination and phrasing of these principles. The Steps were formulated by alcoholics for alcoholics—by and for people suffering from continued, life-damaging behavior—in order to help themselves and others like them overcome that behavior, recover what they had lost or gain what they had never had, and protect themselves from relapsing into it. In that, and in helping many other people overcome other forms of self-hurtful behavior, the Steps have been effective and successful.

"The world is as we are," says an old Hindu expression.

If I would change what I experience to be the world, then I must change myself. The Steps are helpful in this. They are not punitive or self-abnegating, as is occasionally thought. They are gentle. They are healing and restorative.

As they appear in this chapter, the Steps are worded exactly as they are in the literature of Alcoholics Anonymous—except that the word *underearning* has been substituted for the word *alcohol*, and *underearners* for *alcoholics*.*

There is no single way to work the Steps—that is, to engage with them on an active basis. There is only the way

---

* The Steps are given in their original wording in Appendix B.

that is effective for you. My treatment of them here represents my own reflection on them, and my own experience with them, as they relate to underearning. As a rough guideline, aim to work with a Step for a least one or two full months before moving on to the next one. (This is a *very* rough guideline. Ultimately, you'll rely on your intuition.)

The Steps are:

Step One

"We admitted we were powerless over underearning—that our lives had become unmanageable."

This is immediately offensive to nearly everyone.
"Powerless?"
Nonsense!
"Unmanageable?"
Says who?
Personally, I was repelled by the Step: first when it had the word *alcohol* in it, later when it contained the word *debt*, and still later when it had the word *underearning* in it.

It appears to fly in the face of most of what we've been taught. Where's self-reliance here? Strength? Willpower? Where's self-confidence? Pride? Where's damn near everything we so desperately need, that we've prided ourselves on, that we've been told we must have in order to survive, and that many of us have worked so hard to achieve in ourselves?

The first words in AA's book *Twelve Steps and Twelve Traditions,* right after the First Step is given, are: "Who cares to admit complete defeat? Practically no one, of course. Every natural instinct cries out against the idea of personal powerlessness."

Damn straight they do. (The cry of the ego, or self: "If I am not powerful, I will die!")

So how, in the face of this, can we set aside our initial revulsion long enough to take another, less emotional look at the Step to see if it might mean something other than what we first think, if there might be a way we can work with it? The first word in this Step—in the Twelve Steps—is: *We*. That's an important word. *We* means that you are not alone, regardless of how you might have felt till now; that you are not crazy, hopeless, or doomed. That others, many of them, have known the same pain and the same despair. That we have been here before you. That we are here with you now. That you do not have to try to free yourself from this problem alone.

To *admit* to the problem requires nothing more than to acknowledge that it exists, to stop trying to deny or justify it. This is similar to the surrender we discussed in Chapter 3.

But . . . *powerless?*

Your mama!

Has kind of a sickening, horrible ring, doesn't it? It did to me, anyway. My reluctance to admit to such a thing was caused by the fact that—were it true—it would mean that I was weak, incapable, my situation hopeless; that I was condemned to go on underearning forever, to live in poverty and deprivation. What else could being powerless over underearning possibly mean?

But here lies the paradox we first mentioned in Chapter 3. If I truly *am* an underearner (in my case, a compulsive one), then the only way I can ever become free of the compulsion (or tendency, or impulse, or whatever else you wish to call it) is to admit that it's there and that I am powerless over it. If I deny that I'm powerless, then I'll keep trying to prove that I *do* have power over it, that I can overcome it by sheer strength of character and force of will. And I will keep failing, miserably, again and again.

How I dealt with this Step was to look upon admitting that I was powerless over underearning as admitting that my way of doing things, all that I had tried up to this point, simply hadn't worked. (In the short run, of course, some things had, but in the long run they hadn't—the problem was still there.) Despite my conscious desire and best efforts not to, I kept ending up in the same place.

What about the second part of the Step—admitting "that our lives had become unmanageable"? What would be the point in that, even if it *were* true?

Which, you're certain, it is not. (As I was: I had an apartment, a lover, I put on clean clothes every day, made my bed, and my kids loved me; I ate out in restaurants, went to movies, had a VCR, a computer, and my philodendron was thriving. Where was the unmanageability? You maybe, not me.)

Unmanageable doesn't mean down and out and panhandling in the street. It might, but rarely does. Usually it means a pretty constant sense of financial pressure—trouble with bills, debt—and just as important, probably even more so, it means *internal* unmanageability. Internal unmanageability can be even more devastating than external: It can mean pain, fear, despair; emotional chaos; the battering of relationships; anger, paralysis; an inability to live in the day; confusion, shattered self-esteem, and hopelessness.

The First Step is about hitting bottom—coming to the point where you become so weary of the struggle, where the pain is finally so great, that you are willing to say, "Enough, no more." Where you become willing to go to any length to become free of underearning.

One way I work with this Step is to go over it each morning in my mind, reflecting on what it means. And then, just for one day—this day—conscious that I am an underearner and that my life had become unmanageable:

1. I do not incur a new debt.
2. I do not take work that pays me less than I
   need.
3. I do not say no to money.

Something else I did that was illuminating and helpful was to sit down and write out a history of my earning life, paying particular attention to the ways in which I had evaded, avoided, and deflected money.

I did this one summer afternoon when I was alone in a house in the woods, near the ocean. While I had a general sense of my earning life over the years, I wanted to see clearly, in specific detail, what it looked like from the time when I first began to earn, scarcely into my teens, up to the present. So I got out a pad and a pen, sat down at a table, breathed, relaxed —and almost instantly became nauseated over the prospect of committing the story to paper, where the truth of it would be inescapable. The nausea itself was a revelation.

I went out onto the porch and listened to the birds in the trees a while, watched a heron walking around the edges of the little inlet of water across the road. Then I went back in, and after a moment's reflection, telephoned a friend in the city who was also an underearner and who would probably understand. He wasn't home. So I left a short message on his answering machine, telling him what I had just experienced, saying I would run into him soon, and wishing him well. I don't use the telephone much this way, but I was glad I did then. The first word in the Steps is: *We*.

I wrote out a history of my earning that afternoon—or, more accurately, a history of my underearning. It was unsettling and painful. But in the end it was a good thing to have done. It helped me to see reality: It is the story of an underearner.

To work with this Step, reflect upon it—that is, contemplate it as it relates to particulars in your life—for a few minutes each day for an entire month. Somewhere in that month, tell yourself the story of your own earning or underearning. (Putting it down on paper helps.) Later, if you can bring yourself to do so, tell your story out loud to someone you trust, preferably someone also working to free herself from underearning.

Finally, use any other way you find that proves effective for you. This suggestion applies not just to the First Step, but to all the others as well.

Step Two

"Came to believe that a Power greater than ourselves could restore us to sanity."

Problems again, right off the bat. First, there is no power greater than myself. Second, I am not insane.

Next, please.

Before you dismiss this Step entirely, let's look at it more closely. How does one come to believe anything? Primarily, through experience, thought, and observation. Generally belief is an evolutionary process. (In rare cases, it can be instantaneous, as in the face of what appears to be miraculous event. Also, some people can simply *decide* to believe something, recognizing that nearly all beliefs are decisions; that a belief, by definition, is a decision—a matter of faith, something that cannot be *proved*.)

Approach the Second Step in this fashion: Act as if. Act *as if* it were true, as if you *had* come to believe that a Power greater than yourself could restore you to sanity. (We'll talk about what "sanity" might mean later.) In other words, fake it.

(Not exactly, but close enough.) After a while, you may begin to *feel*—at least at moments, or to a degree—that it is true.

When you observe your emotions, for example, do so from the perspective that there *is* a Power greater than yourself that can restore you to sanity. When you reflect on your life in general and on your earning or money in specific, act as if there *were* such a Power. Frequently we are who we pretend to be; and often, belief overcomes the doubter who observes the practice of faith.

There's another—and merry—point to make about this Step: You *already* believe it.

Many people who would scoff at the Second Step are convinced that, say, psychotherapy in some form or another can or is making their lives better. And really, friends—what is this but a belief that a Power greater than yourself can restore you to sanity?

"Well, I mean *(splutter, splutter)*, I didn't know you were going to define it *that* way. . . ."

You can define a power greater than yourself any way you want to.

"Yeah? Well I don't believe in therapy, either."

Okay, so you believe in Harvard, or democracy, socialism, art, the Supreme Court; or in organic food, your gynecologist, fossil fuels, or the Bill of Rights; or in the pastor of the little church around the corner, sleeping with the windows open, or truth, justice, and the American way.

A few years ago, I was on an island in the Gulf of Mexico. It was catching the periphery of a hurricane that was moving from Mexico toward Texas. I went out into the surf, which was gray and brownish and moving in great, heaving swells. For the fun of it, I tried standing against these swells as they loomed up at me. What they did was knock me down and tumble me over and over in toward the beach. I was utterly and completely powerless over them.

So I have no problem, in principle, in conceiving of a power greater than myself. In fact, as I look around, I find that I'm not very powerful at all. Certainly I can influence some aspects of some events connected to my life, but that doesn't constitute having power—not in any real sense of the word. Certainly not to a degree that would cause me to exclude the possibility that there could be a power in the universe greater than myself.

In working the Second Step, start by taking ten minutes to determine—formally—whether you, in the sense of your ego, your personality, what you normally conceive of as your "self," are the most powerful force in the universe.

Me, I wasn't.

So now I can concede that there is a Power in the universe greater than myself (defined any way I like). What then, is this stuff about "restore us to sanity"? Who's insane?

Sanity comes from the Latin *sanus*, "healthy." *Insanity*, on an elemental level, means "not healthy." Performing a self-destructive act, such as getting drunk night after night, is not healthy. Performing *any* self-destructive act is not healthy. It is, in a very basic sense, insane. Repeated underearning, in this sense, can be said to be not sane.

And while *I* may be sane, my compulsion to underearn, or my predilection or inclination to underearn, is not. It is not a healthy thing within me.

And as an antibiotic is something more powerful than anything I'm capable of mustering on my own that can restore a part of me that is not healthy to health, just so, I can accept that some other power greater than myself can restore some other aspect of me that is not healthy to health.

One day, after years of consuming large amounts of alcohol and drugs and in the end being unable to stop, I walked into a room where there were thirty or forty people who had once used drugs and alcohol the same way I was, and who now did not, and suddenly I did not have to drink or take drugs any longer. Whatever I encountered there was certainly a power greater than myself that could restore me to sanity—even if it was nothing but the combined experience and goodwill of the people in that room.

I no longer have to underearn anymore, either.

When are you finished with the Second Step? In a sense, one is never finished with any of the Steps; for many people, working, or living the Steps becomes an ongoing process. But regardless of whether you eventually choose such a course or prefer simply to go through them once, do make at least one formal, progressive trip through them, completing each one before moving on to the next. You're finished with the Second Step when it seems to you, more often than not, that something greater or more effective than you—or than your previous way of doing things—can bring about a healthier state in your life regarding the way you deal with money and experience that life.

Step Three

"Made a decision to turn our will and our lives over to the care of God <u>as we understood Him</u>."

Now I'm *really* leaving.

God was not only a concept but even a *word* that was simply unacceptable to me. I had been militantly an atheist for years. Still, as I mentioned previously, nearly everyone I saw in recovery who had something that I wanted—joy, peace, delight, the ability to get up in the morning with a sense of anticipation rather than thinking "Oh, Christ, it's another day"—had also, on some level or another, something they called a spiritual connection, of some kind or another.

I am a pragmatist. I do what works. And my way was not working well. I began to see that if I wished to live with any kind of equanimity in this new life I was leading, without alcohol and drugs, without debt, and later, without underearning, then sooner or later I would have to deal in some way with the Steps, with the word *God*. This was not a happy recognition.

In the end the key to this Step lay for me in the phrase: "God <u>as we understood Him</u>."

As we understood Him.

Or Her. Or It. Or any other modification that represents an individual understanding. This is clearly not a jealous God —certainly not one in whose name you can go out and bash unbelievers or even believers with a different form of it than you.

If you don't have a god of your understanding, do this:

1. Sit down with a pad.
2. Write out a short description of what, if you could create one, would be an ideal God or Higher Power for you.
3. Accept what you have written as your Higher Power, as "God as you understand Him."

Because it is as valid as any other understanding of God may be.

Tom, an optician, had been raised in a fundamentalist household with a violent, punishing God. He agonized over the Third Step. He *knew* he was corrupt and that God hated him and would continue to punish him until somehow he was able to become perfect, without sin—which he knew with nearly suicidal despair that he never could be. Tom was an underearner of the worst magnitude, deeply in debt, always in torment, barely able to pay his rent each month, and perpetually behind in his child support (which caused him even more pain, since he loved his children deeply). He said he couldn't create a Higher Power this way, because it wouldn't really be God as he understood Him, but only God as he would like Him to be.

But it was pointed out to Tom that the vicious, smiting God of his past was not the God of his understanding either; it was the God of his youthful experience, of his *fear*. Once Tom began to see this, that that God was one he had inherited from someone else, it became easier for him to try working with his own concept of what an ideal Higher Power might be, a God of his desire rather than one of his fear.

Alternatively, borrow someone else's Higher Power. Paula, the acting coach, had a vague image of God as distant, abandoning, and mostly indifferent. For purposes of this Step, she borrowed Jim's Higher Power. Jim, a production supervisor, perceived God as generous and loving. So Paula borrowed his God whenever she worked this Step, or prayed or meditated. In time, Jim's concept began to supplant her own.

The Third Step was a great difficulty for me. In grappling with it, I finally developed for myself the following definition of God or a Higher Power:

What is best in me and best in other people.

The Step then read: "Made a decision to turn our will and our lives over to the care of what is best in us and best in other people."

I could work with that.

Since that time, my concept of God or a Higher Power—whatever there may be—has evolved and continues to evolve. It is now for me less an intellectual definition than an experiential one.

Another important element in Step Three is the word *care*.

The Step suggests that we turn our will and our life over to the *care* of God as we understand God—not to the *tyranny*, *whim*, or *caprice* of God, but to the *care* of God: to the concern, tender regard, affection, and protection of God.

Practice the Third Step by taking a moment, whenever you grow agitated, to become still. Then consciously, without reservation if you can, turn your will and your life over to the care of whatever Higher Power you perceive there to be.

There is no clear marker by which you can know when it is appropriate for you to move from the Third Step to the Fourth. (Leaving a Step behind does not mean that you abandon it, only that your focus shifts to the next one. For some people, the Third Step is a daily—even hourly—practice regardless of what Step they are working on.) Consider yourself ready whenever something solid shifts within you, even if only for an instant, and you feel that you have moved across some sort of threshold, no matter how quickly you might have stepped back. Or when you realize that for several days you have been engaging with the Third Step almost reflexively in the face of small incidents and difficulties.

Step Four

"Made a searching and fearless moral inventory of ourselves."

Some people reject this Step out of hand. The problem is with the word *moral*, which can be a charged one. I first read the Step to mean: "Came up with an exhaustive list of all the ways we were sinful, corrupt, and wrong."

And to have done that would have been to depress myself even further than I already was. The Step seemed little more than an invitation to self-hatred. When finally I did approach the Step, I found it helpful to look at it from back to front, beginning with the word *inventory*.

An inventory is just that, an inventory—it is *not* a bill of indictment or a catalog of all the ways in which you are a rotten human being. When a store owner takes an inventory, he makes an objective, nonjudgmental survey of all the goods and materials he has in stock. That's all a personal inventory is: an objective, nonjudgmental survey of what you have in stock. It's essential for your inventory to be balanced, for it to include what is positive about you as well as what is negative. A store inventory doesn't list just the broken television sets in stock—it lists *all* the television sets, broken *and* working. An inventory simply says: This is what is.

But why, then, this word *moral?* I wish I had a snappy, one-line response, but I don't. If you want to approach morality from the perspective of some childhood orthodoxy you were taught—hanging your head, beating your breast—then go ahead. I don't think that's very productive. What I did was to disconnect the word *moral* from any sense of judgment, of sin or virtue. Instead, I looked upon it to mean the difference between what was helpful to me or harmful, what was constructive in my life or destructive. This helped me to see both myself and the value of the Step more clearly.

If I am strongly impatient, for example, not only will I hurt the feelings of people around me, I will also hurt myself —if at no other level than the pragmatic one of depriving myself of their goodwill and best efforts on my behalf.

The word *searching* was self-explanatory: thorough.

With the word *fearless*, the question was not what, but rather how. One way to help yourself conduct an inventory fearlessly is to do a brief Third Step just beforehand. Get still, and in that stillness make a decision to turn your life and will during this period over to the *care* of God *as you understand God*. Another way is to limit the time you work on the Step to a maximum of half an hour on any one day. This will prevent you from becoming overwhelmed. Set a kitchen timer. When it rings, stop working and put the Step aside. You're finished with it for the day.

There are many ways to do a Fourth Step. Below are two that I and others have found especially effective:

The Three-Criteria Method

Work with a legal-size yellow pad. Draw a vertical line down your sheet of paper, dividing it in half. Label the left-hand column "Negative," the right "Positive." In the Negative column, break your life into manageable units by listing topics. As topics for this column, a list of the Seven Deadly Sins serves well. (We are not using the word *sin* in any theological sense here. We are simply naming fundamental qualities that can damage us.) Across from each, on the right-hand side (Positive), balance the negative quality with what you think of as its opposite. This is how such a pairing might look:

Negative	*Positive*
Pride	Humility
Greed	Generosity
Lust	*Caritas* (selfless love)
Anger	Kindness
Gluttony	Temperateness
Envy	Celebration
Sloth	Energy

After you've made the list, begin by working through the first topic on the Negative side. When you're finished, go over to the Positive side and work through the balancing topic there. Then proceed to the next Negative one, and continue in this fashion.

What does it mean to "work through" a topic? It means, under that heading, to search your life as far back as you can remember for incidents that relate to the heading. Pride, for example, or Greed. On the opposite side, Humility or Generosity. When you work through a topic on the Negative side, look for all the things you did related to it that fit one or more of these three criteria, that either:

1. You are most ashamed of
2. Make you think less of yourself

or . . .

3. You would least like another human being to know about you

Limit the number of incidents under each topic to no more than ten (unless you feel it is vital to include more). Don't write them out in detail. All you need is a phrase or sentence to jog your memory when you see it again; you'll know what the event is.

To illustrate, here's an entry from Barry's Fourth Step— Barry is an attorney—under the topic Pride: *"Smoking in back seat, burned down Brian's car."* That's all he needed in order to acknowledge the incident and be able to recognize it later. Here, as he later explained it, is the incident.

I was seventeen. I owned a car. Every morning I would pick up my girlfriend and three other students (who chipped in for gas) and drive them with me to the township high school, five miles away.

Once when my car needed repairs, I brought it to the garage to leave overnight. I worked out the next morning's transportation with Brian, one of the students I usually drove.

The next morning, Brian picked us all up. He was a little nervous. I was riding in the back seat. I was a heavy smoker then. I lit up. Brian asked me not to smoke. No one in his family did. He didn't want the smell in his car, or ashes. It was winter. I rolled the window partway down and told him I would blow the smoke out the window, flick the ashes out too, and not to worry about it.

"Please!" he said.

I ignored him.

We reached school, parked in the big lot. At about noontime, I heard fire engines outside. I knew in my gut what had happened, even though the news didn't go through the school for another half hour: Brian's car had burned. The fire had started in the back seat.

After school Brian confronted me, angry and crying. I completely denied any responsibility, though I knew I *was* responsible. During the drive that morning, I had thought I saw a red ember blow back in when I flicked the ash from my cigarette outside the window. I had looked for it on the seat, on the floor, didn't find anything, and, in the same spirit in which I had refused Brian's entreaty not to smoke in the car, put it out of mind.

And burned down a family's car. And then lied. Swore I had been meticulously careful with my cigarette. Insisted the fire was simply coincidence.

That was the incident. But all that was necessary for Barry to write was: *"Smoking in back seat, burned down Brian's car."*

Barry put this incident under the heading Pride. His refusal to comply with Brian's request, he felt, had involved arrogance and bullying; his later lying, cowardice and fear—all stemming from his pride. It met not just one but all of the criteria under which he was conducting his inventory: He was ashamed of what he had done, his behavior made him think less of himself, and he would be embarrassed to have anyone else know the truth of what had happened.

When working through a topic on the Positive side, search your memory for incidents in which you acted primarily out of *that* quality. Kindness, for example. Or Celebration. Celebration might involve your true pleasure in someone else's happy event—perhaps even one you'd like for yourself, such as a marriage, or promotion—and your contributing to their further happiness by congratulating them or in some other way. Here, take note too of ways in which you usually behave or feel. Under Generosity, for example, you might put down: "I truly like getting presents for people." Or: "When I was in college, I was usually happy to help other students who needed help with their studies." Or: "I'm genuinely pleased for people when they get free of something that's been troubling them." Again, limit the number of your entries to no more than ten.

Do the topics in pairs, first the Negative one, then, on the Positive side, its balancing opposite. When you finish one pair, go on to the next. How much time people put into making an inventory of this kind varies. Generally you can do a thorough job by spending between half an hour and an hour on each topic. Since there are fourteen topics—the Seven Deadly Sins and their opposites—that means a total of seven to fourteen hours.

The Resentment Method

This second way of doing a Fourth Step is a variation of a traditional method in the book *Alcoholics Anonymous*. It helps us see the role that we ourselves played in incidents over which we feel angry or aggrieved, and why we played that role.

This method requires a little mechanical preparation. Using a ruler or straight-edge, set up a piece of typing paper by drawing lines on it so that it looks something like this:

Then print a heading for each column across the top, so that the top row reads this way:

Name	Why I Resent Him/Her	What That Incident Threatened In Me	What My Part In It Was (Is)	What I Could Have Done (or Can Do) Differently

At a copy shop have as many copies made of this form as you think you might need. (There is room for four names on each sheet.)

Here's how to work with the Resentment Method:

(Before each session you might want do a brief Third Step, so that you know you're in the care of whatever Higher Power you perceive there to be while you're working on this. Restrict the time you spend on each session to no more than half an hour. Slow, steady progress will get a Fourth Step done more quickly, more thoroughly, and with less emotional difficulty than will lunging at it at irregular intervals.)

First, list the name of every person toward whom you feel resentful. Then every institution. List *all* your resentments, in the first column of as many pages as it takes.

(Within reason: If you feel you have a horde of resentments, you might be mistaking irritation for resentment. Set a maximum number of twenty-five names. If you have more resentments than that, pick the twenty-five you feel the most intensely. You can always work the remaining ones later if you wish. Some people, at the opposite pole, may have only half a dozen or so, or even—though rarely—fewer.)

When you're finished listing the names, return to the first page. Now, after each name, in the second column—"Why I Resent Him/Her" (or It)—write down a phrase that describes the cause of your resentment. Try not to use emotional words such as "He screwed me over" or "She's a lying bitch." These tend only to agitate you and color or obscure the event. Instead, keep your description to a simple declaration of fact. For example: "Stole my silver lighter." Or: "Divorced me." "Beat me up." "Never says hello to me." "Did bad work on my teeth that I had to get done over."

Go through your entire list this way, writing down the reason you feel resentful toward each person and institution.

When you've completed that part, return to the first page again. Now, one name at a time, look at the reason you feel resentful toward this person or institution, and then, in the next space, in the third column—"What That Threatened In

Me"—write down what was threatened in you by this act. This will nearly always be one of five major elements: your self-esteem, personal relationships, security (financial, emotional, or physical), sexuality, or ambition (material, social, or sexual). Most of our resentments can be traced to threats to one or more of these. As best you can, identify what was or is being threatened in you in each case. Here is an entry from a Fourth Step done by Joanie, an editor:

Name	Why I Resent Him/Her	What That Incident Threatened In Me	What My Part In It Was (Is)	What I Could Have Done (or Can Do) Differently
Ted	Divorced me	Self-esteem Emotional security Financial security Sexual life Financial & social ambition		

Go through your entire list in this fashion.

Next, return one final time to the beginning. Now fill out the last two columns after each name—"What My Part In It Was (Is)" and "What I Could Have Done (or Can Do) Differently." Do them simultaneously. This is how Joanie continued:

Name	Why I Resent Him/Her	What That Incident Threatened In Me	What My Part In It Was (Is)	What I Could Have Done (or Can Do) Differently
Ted	Divorced me	Self-esteem Emotional security Financial security Sexual life Financial & social ambition	My drinking My jealousy My going to bed with other men That I didn't tell him from the start of the trouble that I wanted to stay married	Told him I wanted to stay married. Been faithful to him. Gone for marital counseling. Recognized we both had a problem with alcohol. Stayed in the house, not left in anger and taken an apartment.

When you fill out the fourth column, deal only with *your* part in the event, not the other person's. Do not, for example, put down, "I kicked in the door because she locked me out." This is denial and self-justification. It may be true that she locked you out. It may be true that you needed your brown suit for a business meeting in the morning. It may be true, in fact, that she was ninety percent responsible for the sequence of events that led to your getting arrested and hauled off to spend the night in jail. But in doing this inventory we are interested only in what *our* part in the incident was, what *we* contributed to bringing it about. This is a searching and fearless inventory of *ourselves*, not everyone else. So simply recognize that your act of kicking down the door did play a part—and possibly even the major part—in your being arrested and taken away by the police. That's all we're looking for here—recognition of our part.

In the final column, "What I Could Have Done Differently," deal only with what you *could* have done that might have had a positive effect on the outcome—not what you think you *should* have done, or *wanted* to do. Instead of kicking in the door, for example, you could have: Apologized. Asked if she would hand your suit out through the door to you. Called her sister and requested her to intervene. Changed your business appointment. Or a variety of other things, according to your actual situation.

Now it's true that kicking the door down might have been exactly what you *wanted* to do. And that even if you had tried any of the alternatives, or even all of them, the outcome might still have been more or less the same. But the point of thinking about this and filling in this column is to make ourselves aware that there *were* options, that we *could* have acted in a different manner—which might have brought about a happier result. Go through your entire list, putting down what your part in each incident was and what you might have done differently.

Justified Resentments

On rare occasion there is a situation in which resentment—even raging, white-hot, hate-filled resentment—seems thoroughly justified. Not only to the person who holds it, but to

Why Do Any of This at All?

Making a Fourth Step inventory of any kind will probably stir up some painful memories or emotions in you. Nearly everyone who makes an inventory will—at the least—wince a few times. Why, then, subject yourself to such a process?

Because the material an inventory brings forward is within you anyway. It works at you, influencing your emotions and behavior, even if you are not consciously aware of it. And the more ignorant of this material you remain, the less capable you are of managing your life, effecting the kind of changes you'd like to, and freeing yourself from underearning.

It is here that the roots of underearning lie.

As a football coach, you would be hopelessly disadvantaged by not knowing the strengths and weaknesses of your team. You couldn't hope to win very often or even guess what you might do to improve your team. When you don't know the strengths and weaknesses of your own "self," you are pretty much in the same position.

In General

Do a broad Fourth Step first—one that covers your entire life. Later you can do smaller inventories, if you wish, focusing on areas with which you're having trouble, such as family or relationships.

I strongly suggest that you do at least one of these smaller, focused inventories on the subject: *Money.* The Resentment Method is especially suited to this. Write down the name of every person and institution toward whom you feel resentment over something involving money. Then work through the rest of the columns as described above.

People who've been in psychotherapy sometimes think the Fourth Step is irrelevant to them, that they've covered this ground already. But they haven't, as anyone experienced with both therapy and the Fourth Step clearly knows. Painting and writing are both art forms, but different arts. Therapy is not a replacement for a Fourth Step.

A Word About Guilt

The toxic material you may dredge up in an inventory can be harmful to carry around in your consciousness for an extended period of time. It can eat at you, tempt you toward guilt or self-loathing. Neither of these is desirable. Both are counterproductive. Neither has anything to do with recognition, acceptance of responsibility, and regret—which are healthy.

The Fifth Step, which follows, is in part a way to prevent guilt or self-loathing. Ideally, you'll arrange to do a Fifth Step within a few days of completing your Fourth Step.

(Also, by the time you undertake a Fourth Step, you'll be less vulnerable to guilt or self-loathing because of the preceding Steps you've worked and many of Prospering's other techniques, particularly those from Chapter 8, such as "Becoming Free" and "Having Tea with Your Emotions.")

Doing a Fifth Step requires the cooperation of another human being, someone absolutely trustworthy and who has nothing but your best interests at heart. A Fifth Step is a sharing of yourself and any burden you may have with another human being. If you are delayed in doing it for any reason, you might want to fold your Fourth Step in half, put it into a manila envelope, and put the envelope into your freezer. Keep it there—frozen solid, out of your life—until you're ready to thaw it out and do a Fifth Step.

That's what I did. And it worked.

Step Five

"Admitted to God, to ourselves, and to another human being the exact nature of our wrongs."

By the time many people reach the Fifth Step, they are bristling less about some of the words and concepts in the Steps than they were in the beginning. For others, each Step remains a new hurdle.

It was apparent to me when I first saw this Step that with the word *wrongs* its writers were talking about *sins*—all the evil, corrupt, disgusting things I had supposedly done in my life for which I could scarcely be forgiven, by either God or man, and for which, except for the benevolent caprice of God's mercy, I would burn in hell throughout eternity; for which, as I had been taught, I *deserved* to burn. So I knew what this Step was about. I had a lot of experience with that kind of thing.

Except that I didn't really know. What I had been taught in my childhood was something entirely different from what the Fifth Step means. When I arrived at the Fifth Step after having worked through the first four, I did not see it the same way.

With the Fifth Step, as with the Fourth, I was helped by looking at it from back to front.

Wrongs?

Mistakes, errors, acts that were inappropriate. Things that did not work for my own good, that, in the end, hurt me. Incidents I was ashamed of, that made me think less of myself, that I would least like another human being to know about me. Resentments, which are harmful to me.

Their *exact nature?*

I took this to mean an objective, accurate account of the incidents I had written down in my Fourth Step, the resentments I had explored.

Why admit these *to God, to ourselves, and to another human being*?

Because, on all counts, it is a profound and liberating thing to do. Sitting down with another human being and admitting to him or her—and by that act to ourselves, without reservation, and to God—the exact nature of our wrongs releases and heals us at the deepest, most significant levels of our being.

Without such release, these mistakes, errors, and resentments, these things we are ashamed of, that make us think less of ourselves, that we fear other people coming to know about us, can—and often do—poison us from within. We have to spend a great amount of psychic energy trying to repress or justify them. We feel shame, anger, and guilt; our sense of isolation increases. All of which damage us in general and contribute to our continued underearning.

Nearly everyone who does a Fifth Step experiences this sense of release and healing. For some, it is immediate and can be almost overpowering. For others, it is not.

"I myself felt only a bit of relief as I walked back out into the street after finishing my Fifth Step," says Joanie, the divorced editor. "In fact, it was a little disappointing. But what happened was that the effect continued to reverberate within me for nearly a year. Its impact was cumulative. Month by month, I experienced a lightening of my being. I became freer and freer from images and memories that had oppressed me for years, that had sometimes slashed into my consciousness with such pain that I would gasp. It was only in retrospect that I became aware that many of these had left me, and that my experience of the ones that remained was less frequent and their effect less powerful."

Pick the person with whom you intend to do your Fifth Step carefully. Be sure it is someone trustworthy and understanding, who can comprehend the purpose of what you are doing. It should not be your spouse or any other relative—family dynamics can be difficult here. Also, since you'll be sharing intimate material with this person, it should be someone of the same sex or at least with whom there is no possibility of attraction. If possible, make it someone experienced with the Steps and who has completed a Fifth Step of his own. If you don't know such a person, you can probably find one with a little ingenuity. Ask trusted friends if they know someone, ask your clergyman or therapist, or call your local community health center.

Someone who has done a Fifth Step of her own (and ideally been the recipient of other people's Fifth Steps) brings valuable experience and understanding to your process. She may share with you a bit of her own history that is similar to what you're describing, which can help you realize that you are neither alone nor uniquely terrible. She also knows the importance of not making judgmental comments ("Wow, that's disgusting!") or dismissive ones ("I don't see why you're so upset about that"). She can, if appropriate, gently try to help you see a particular event in perspective. But still, the primary role of the listener is to serve as witness—attentive and compassionate. She is not there to judge you or disqualify you.

Some people can't bring themselves to admit the incidents from their Fourth Step to anyone but their clergyman or therapist. That's fine. Eventually, though, most of them find that this was unsatisfactory and decide to do another Fifth Step with someone like themselves, who is also getting free from underearning.

The simplest way to do a Fifth Step is to share with whomever is receiving it the Fourth Step inventory you wrote using the Three-Criteria Method. This can be a good, general clearing out. Later you can do other, smaller Fifth Steps if you wish, on specific subjects or resentments.

Step Six

"Were entirely ready to have God remove all these defects of character."

These *what?*

Defects of character.

Here is yet another phrase to alarm and offend. It suggests that I am defective; it implies—to me, at least—that I am unacceptable. "No good. Reject. Next!" And I'm out in the trash barrel.

But that is not what this Step is about. A defect is nothing more than a flaw or an imperfection.

Even if I am highly imperfect, scored by a multitude of defects, that does not mean that *I* am defective, wrong, somehow no good. No more than a car is defective, or wrong, or somehow no good, because it has a defective turn signal. It is simply a car with a defective turn signal. If the defect were removed, the car would be easier to operate and less likely to cause damage to itself or anyone else.

So a defect of character is something that does not work well within me, that causes me trouble; an obstacle to my living as well as I might; something, basically, that hurts or can hurt me.

Okay, so what are *these* defects?

Essentially, what I came up with in my Fourth Step: the fear, anger, and pridefulness, what in the literature of AA is called "instincts run wild," and the behaviors that resulted from these. Your Fourth Step may have revealed to you, for example, that you have a tendency to lie or to feel justified in petty theft, to a degree that has caused you to do things you are ashamed of, that make you think less of yourself, or that you wouldn't want another human being to know about you. These and the others are your immediately apparent defects, the major obstacles within you to your living happily and prosperously.

"All right," you might say. "That seems reasonable." (You might not, but I will.) "How do I go about removing these defects?"

You, personally, *don't*. The Step doesn't say anything about you removing your defects. It talks about being ready to have God remove them.

If you have a God or Higher Power of some sort, you probably won't have much trouble with this part of the Step. (Unless you think your God would never do such a thing for you. In that case, borrow someone else's.) If you don't have a God and aren't interested in anyone else's, even temporarily, you can *still* be entirely ready for God to remove these defects. Remember, it's *God as we understood Him*, as *you* understand Him (Her, It, Mind, Energy).

God as I understood God was what was best in me and others. Who could possibly object to what is best in him removing from his character everything that stands as an obstacle to him living a happy, prosperous life? (If *you* can, I stand confounded before you.)

So maybe you're willing to become entirely ready to have God as you understand Him remove these defects of character. How do you go about doing that?

In two ways.

First, by not incurring any new debt one day at a time,* by not taking work that pays you less than you need, and by not saying no to money.

It is impossible to become entirely ready to have your defects of character removed if you are consciously underearn-

---

* There are occasional exceptions to this, but only among the few underearners who have never had trouble of *any* kind with debt. Be extremely careful in deciding if this applies to you. Incurring any amount of unsecured debt is lethal to the recovery of nearly all underearners.

ing. Just as it is impossible for an alcoholic to become entirely ready to have his defects of character removed if he continues to drink. Your continued underearning acts like a impenetrable wall between you and whatever kind of Higher Power you perceive there to be.

The second way to become entirely ready is to work the previous five Steps.

In fact, it's difficult to become entirely ready without doing this. In my own case, I would never have gone to the effort of working any of the later Steps if I hadn't done the first one —admitted I was powerless over underearning and that my life had become unmanageable. Then, in order to trust that I *could* be freed from this habit, or affliction, I needed to believe that a power greater than myself—whatever that might be—could restore me to sanity. Then, deciding to turn my will and my life over to the care of that power gave me a sense of safety, comfort, and confidence that helped me continue. By doing an inventory, I gained an idea of what my defects were. And finally, to help myself see them clearly, realize they didn't make me hideous or wrong, and accept them, I admitted to a Higher Power, to myself, and to another human being the exact nature of my wrongs. Having done those Steps, I arrived at the Sixth Step largely ready to have a higher power remove my defects of character.

Largely—not *entirely*.

I was mystified as to how to continue. Nor was I certain that I wanted to have *all* my defects removed. Who would I be without occasionally bringing cutting wit into play? How could I stand up for myself without my pride? How could I keep the predators at bay without my anger?

I returned again and again to the preceding Steps. I spoke with people who were experienced with the Sixth Step. I worked the other techniques and disciplines of Prospering.

And I did one other thing that was helpful too. Several

nights each week, just before I went to sleep (or sometimes during the day, in a small meditation), I would relax my body, become still, and then summon from within myself as much sincere and genuine willingness to have all these defects of character removed as I could. Sometimes this wasn't very much, and usually I could sustain the willingness, no matter how much or how little, for only a moment or two. But it was all that I knew to do, and intuitively I sensed its rightness—for me, anyway.

I did this for about three months. In the latter stages it became easier for me to muster, if not complete willingness, then something at least close to that. As a variation, I sometimes worked toward becoming willing to have God remove from me not only all the character defects of which I was aware but all those of which I might be unaware. And in yet another variation—less often, and quite frightening when I first did it—to be willing to have God remove from me everything that was not God. After a while, now and then, I would experience a fractional instant—a *millisecond*, gone nearly as quickly as it had come—of complete willingness. But these half-dozen or so times did not leave me with the sense that I had become entirely ready. So I continued.

One evening around nine o'clock, I lay down on the carpet in my living room, relaxed, became still, and went through this exercise again. What I did and felt was fairly ordinary. There was nothing to separate this session from the large number of other times I had done the exercise. Yet when I opened my eyes a few minutes later, breathed, stretched, and stood up, I knew I was finished with the Sixth Step, that I was entirely ready to have God remove all these defects of character. There was no white light, no experience of transfiguration, no ecstasy or rapture. All I did was feel good, in a fairly normal way; perhaps slightly quieter than usual, and with a bit more peace.

Whatever. I was finished, and I knew it.

In time, I would be ready to move to the Seventh Step. As will you.

No principle separates the first six Steps from the last. I've divided them in half simply to provide a break, a kind of psychological stand-up-and-stretch. At this point in your reading you might want to stand up physically and stretch—or even take a rest for a day or two. I certainly recommend that when you actually *work* the Steps—if you choose to—you take anywhere from a couple of days to a couple of weeks off after finishing one before you move on to the next. Doing that will refresh you and make your work with the next Step even more satisfying and effective.

9.

STEPS SEVEN THROUGH TWELVE

THIS CHAPTER CONTAINS THE LAST SIX OF THE TWELVE STEPS as they were originated in Alcoholics Anonymous and ways to work with them to help free yourself from underearning. As in Chapter 8, the term *underearners* has been substituted for *alcoholics*.

Step Seven

"Humbly asked Him to remove our shortcomings."

The Seventh Step seems simple enough, and actually is—though what is simple is not necessarily easy.

Once again it may be useful to take this Step from back to front. Why are the defects, as they were called in the Sixth Step, now called *shortcomings*? Frankly, I don't know. Perhaps, since there is a slight connotative difference between the two, the intent was to soften the impact of the word *defect*. Or maybe it was just to avoid redundancy. I don't think there is any deep significance here. Whatever the explanation, we end up with the defects of the Sixth Step being the shortcomings of the Seventh Step. In the Sixth Step we became entirely ready to have God remove them.

Here in the Seventh Step we humbly ask Him to do so— *Him* being whatever you understand to be a Higher Power. Even if you're a strict empiricist, it still shouldn't be too difficult for you to humbly ask something larger than yourself— say, what's best in you and best in other people—to remove your shortcomings.

Well, *ideally* it shouldn't be hard.

The *humbly* part causes trouble for some people. (Most, actually.) It's hard for many of us to differentiate humility from humiliation. Let's settle for this: To be humble is to present oneself without pride, pretense, or arrogance. To be humiliated is to be shamed, debased, or degraded. There's a world of difference between the two.

To ask humbly means to ask with the recognition that whatever you perceive a Higher Power to be, it is something larger or more powerful or more effective than your own ego or self. To ask with the understanding that you are not the alpha and omega of the universe. To ask without arrogance or vanity—quietly, from your true and peaceful heart.

Let's assume you can do that, that you can humbly ask whatever you define a Higher Power to be to remove your shortcomings. The question then is, *will* it?

In my experience, and in what I have observed in others over the years, yes. What some people call "The Promises" appear in the Big Book of AA, after the discussion of the Ninth Step. The promises are a brief list of what can be expected "if we are painstaking about this phase of our development," meaning working the first nine Steps. One of the promises says: "We will suddenly realize that God is doing for us what we could not do for ourselves."

(If you're uncomfortable with that, you can translate it to read, "We will suddenly realize that our higher self is doing for us what our ego—or our fearful, angry, or arrogant self—could not." Or in some other fashion.)

This too, in my experience and observation, is true.

For me, an important qualifying phrase in this Step, is *what we could not do for ourselves.* In my case, whatever I understand a Higher Power to be, while being perfectly willing to do for me what I cannot do for myself, apparently won't do a single thing for me that I *can* do for myself. That at least has been my experience. In other words, this is never a free lunch —we have to do our part.

So after you have done everything you're capable of to help yourself (and if you've worked the previous Steps, and the other parts of Prospering, you probably have), and you now humbly ask a Higher Power as you understand it to remove your shortcomings, how might it do that?

Instantly. Or at the end of the day. Or over a long period of time. Forever. Or for a month, an hour, or only a few minutes. By direct and recognized divine intervention (whatever that means to you), or by your encountering a good therapist, or through reading some sentences in a book, or the birth of a child, a phone call, or a conversation overheard in a restaurant. In as many ways as you can imagine and a great many more that you can't, a God as you understand God, or a Higher Power as you understand it, might remove your shortcomings.

They'll be removed, that's all.

Mine—some, anyway—have been removed in various ways. Others remain. Still others have been only partly removed, or have been removed only to return and then be removed again. Some I have to ask every day to be removed.

How does one ask? Some people suggest that after working through the first six Steps, all that's left to do is to pick a
quiet afternoon, sit down, become still, and say, "God, please
remove my shortcomings." Others go to a church, temple, or
zendo to make a kind of private ceremony of asking. Do
whichever of these feels right to you, or anything else your
intuition provides you with.

Some years ago, I was in New York working as a consulting editor for a newspaper. I had recently returned from Florida, where I had lived briefly while helping launch a new
magazine and where I had started a group where people who
had a problem with debt could come to help themselves. Now,
back in New York, I received a call one morning at the paper
from a woman who'd been part of that group. There was
stress in her voice. She said, "Katie was raped last night."

I grunted—shocked, hurt.

Katie, a woman in her early twenties, had been raped twice
as a child. I liked her and had worked with her in the debt
group. Guarded at first, she'd been making good strides
toward trusting people.

The night before, a guy in a van had cut her off while she
was on her bicycle, dragged her into the van at knifepoint, and
raped her.

After we hung up, the anger that had been building in me
through the conversation blossomed into rage. Pure, burning, murderous rage. Crazed, all-encompassing, hate-filled
rage.

I wanted to kill this man who had raped Katie. I wanted
to terrorize him, as he had terrorized her. I saw myself holding him by his shirt front. He was tall, wore dirty jeans, had a
day's stubble on his cheeks, with lank, unwashed hair. I
jammed the barrel of a gun I own into his mouth. His eyes
were wide with horror. I was saying, in a voice so low and
furious I could hardly get the words out, "Now, motherfucker,

now how does it feel?" Telling him the magnitude of what he had done to this young woman, then saying, joyfully, fiercely: "Now *die*, motherfucker!" And blowing the top of his head off.

I could not control this rage. It was overpowering every part of me.

From the calm vantage of today, as I write these words, was my feeling justified? Did this man deserve to die, or at least to be punished in some severe way? Those, though it may be difficult to see at first, are irrelevant questions. The point is: *I* was being devoured by this mad rage. *I* was the one being hurt.

I could scarcely think, only confusedly. I couldn't function, sit at my desk, deal with the people around me. The damage I was sustaining began to spread; my state was now affecting others, who couldn't help but notice that something not good was happening within me. I went out of the area in which I worked and into the building's large cafeteria, where I sat in a corner by myself and tried to deal with this. But I couldn't.

I tried blessing this man—not his act, him—but couldn't. I tried praying for him, but couldn't. I tried forgiving him, but couldn't. All I *could* do was feel this rage, so strong that at moments I would jerk with it.

Justified or not, my rage was wholly destructive—to me, to the people around me, and to the paper, which was paying me for time and services I was incapable of giving it now. And justified or not, my rage was contributing nothing toward the capture and punishment of the man who had done this, or toward comforting Katie.

So, needing help, I called another editor at the paper, whom I knew a little and who lived the kind of life that I had been living for the past few years. He listened, understanding. "You're right," he said. "You *can't* pray for the bastard. You *can't* bless him. You *can't* forgive him." He paused. "Jerry . . . are you powerless over this rage?"

I was breathing hard, beginning to get angry at him, fearing the direction in which he might be going. "Yes," I said.

"Okay," he said. "So there's nothing you can do about it. That's what we're looking at: You are absolutely powerless over this rage." He paused again, then said, "And if you can't do anything about it, are you willing to let God remove it?"

"No. Yes. I don't know."

"Whatever you want is all right. Just know that you have a choice. If you do want to have it removed—if you're ready— then ask. Just say, 'I can't do this. I'd appreciate it if You would,' or anything else you want."

Not long after, I did as he suggested. I went into the fire-stairwell, sat on a step, put my face in my hands, and—though I was still burning with the rage—became entirely ready to have it removed; asked to have it removed.

And it was. I felt some abatement immediately, though only a little. The emptying continued over the next two hours, and my capacity to function steadily increased until—while a residue of anger remained and would occasionally flare up—I was free of it.

What I learned that day was that I could use the Seventh Step in specific situations as well as on a broad, general level. So now in the present, when I recognize that a shortcoming or defect is at play and that I am powerless over it, I ask to have it removed—if I'm entirely ready.

That is a problem sometimes. You'd think that we would always be willing or ready to have something that is hurting us removed. But I'm not, and nor has anyone else I've ever known. Sometimes I know the reason: I may feel justified in my sense of aggrievedness, for example, and fear that if I surrender it I won't get redress. But other times I don't.

Debbie, a photographer, had just learned that her arrangement with a magazine conglomerate as an independent contractor was being canceled and that she was going to drop from making $1,000 a week to making nothing a week in less than a month. "I was experiencing an attack of fear," she said. "It had become intense. Reflexively, as I was crossing a corner, I began a combination Sixth and Seventh Step over the fear. To my astonishment I discovered—and almost tripped over my own feet in the middle of the street because of it—that I was *not* ready to have the fear removed. What's more, I didn't even *want* to be ready. I wanted to hang on to that fear, miserable as it made me feel. I don't know why; it makes no sense. Yet there it was: I didn't *want* the fear to be removed.

"That discovery itself was of some help. At least I knew I was exercising choice in the matter. I didn't know anything else to do but accept that I wasn't ready. So I thought, Okay, we'll try again later and see what happens then. Half an hour later, I *was* entirely ready. I asked, and the fear was removed. It popped back a few times over the next couple of weeks, but it was nothing I couldn't handle."

What, it might be asked, do emotions such as I experienced and that Debbie experienced have to do with underearning—especially when they may seem appropriate to the situation?

Underearning does not take place in a vacuum. It is the result of the activity of various aspects of our "self"—particularly negative aspects, such as fear and anger. While it may not be difficult for some people to stop underearning, *staying* stopped is often much harder. The only way to ensure continuing freedom from underearning—especially for a chronic or compulsive underearner—is through this kind of inner work, the establishment of a deep equilibrium. Can one liberate oneself from underearning for the long term without doing so? Probably. But I think that would be very difficult and much less pleasurable. What's more, freedom from such experiences and emotions—or at least being able to deal with them effectively—is ultimately also a part of living prosperously.

(Such freedom doesn't mean you won't feel them sometimes. It means you won't be tyrannized by them.)

Here is a way I used the Seventh Step to work *directly* on my underearning. I undertook it every morning during the first year of my liberation, and I still do occasionally now. I suggest it to you. Becoming still, with my eyes closed, I say the First Step silently to myself ("Admitted we were powerless over underearning—that our lives had become unmanageable"). Then I reflect on the Step (*be* with it, which is hard to explain; simply involve yourself with it in whatever way seems the most complete) for about a minute. Next, I say the Second Step ("Came to believe that a Power greater than ourselves could restore us to sanity") and reflect on or be with it for a minute. Then I say the Third Step ("Made a decision to turn our will and our lives over to the care of God *as we understood Him*") and be with it. From there I go to the Sixth Step, saying "this defect" rather than "these defects" ("Were entirely ready to have God remove this defect of character") and reflect on it. Then, ending, I move to the Seventh Step, saying "this shortcoming" instead of "our shortcomings" ("Humbly asked Him to remove this shortcoming"); and then I ask, humbly, in confidence, and with gratitude, for the compulsion to underearn to be removed from me.

And one day at a time—though I've had to do the part that is mine and still do— it has.

Step Eight

"Made a list of all persons we had harmed, and became willing to make amends to them all."

This Step is pretty straightforward—and stops some people cold.

But it is as important as any of the others, even if its relation to underearning is not immediately apparent. The knowledge of these harmful events is already within you. And no matter how strongly you may have tried to justify them or how deeply you might have buried them, your emotions over them—the guilt, the remorse, even on a subconscious level—and the mental formulations you have created around them, the arguments, equivocations, and the energy you expend on them, all contribute to your underearning, are part of the cause. You need to get free of these in order to strengthen your liberation and help it to become lasting.

The people who have the most trouble with this Step are usually those who perceive themselves as having been more harmed in life than harmful, or who believe that the only one they ever truly harmed was themselves. Others, while willing to grant that they might indeed have harmed some people, can't imagine ever embarrassing themselves by making amends. Still others refuse even to consider making amends to a given person because of the hurt that person inflicted on them. We'll address each of these situations later. First, it will be helpful to approach the Step more generally.

The easiest way to work with the Eighth Step is to divide it into two parts:

1. *Made a list of all persons we had harmed, and*
2. *became willing to make amends to them all.*

What constitutes harm? Basically, to hurt, injure, or damage someone in some way. We can harm people physically. We can harm them emotionally. We can harm them psychologically. It's not necessary to leave them dead or dying in the dust to have harmed them; a cutting remark made when someone was vulnerable could have been deeply wounding, have caused emotional or psychological harm.

Most of us fall into one of three groups over this Step:

those quite willing to believe the worst of themselves; those who blame and resent others and insist that they have scarcely ever harmed anyone else; and those open at least to trying to take an honest look at what harm they might or might not have done. Obviously, this last is the only helpful perspective from which to approach the Step.

No matter what kind of harm you have done in your life, you are not a terrible and hurtful human being; you would not be reading a book like this if you were. Nor, conversely, are you someone so gentle, timid, and sweet that you have never harmed another human being. It's not possible to have lived long enough to become an adult without having harmed others along the way.

Making the List

The first part of the Step—*Made a list of all persons we had harmed* —is simple. It involves just that, period. Nothing more than making a list.

Make your list over several days or even weeks, rather than trying to complete it all at once. This will help prevent you from going into overload. Limit any given session on it to half an hour (as you did with the Fourth Step). Set a kitchen timer. Breathe, relax. Say the Third Step to yourself, then start. Be honest as you search your life—neither too quick to find yourself guilty, nor to justify or excuse yourself. When you're uncertain whether you actually harmed someone, use the three criteria from the Fourth Step to help decide. Are you ashamed of this incident? Does it make you think less of yourself? Would you prefer that another human being not know this about you? If the answer is yes to any of these, the name belongs on the list.

There will be situations in which someone else started

the trouble or in which you were hurt much more than you hurt back. Nevertheless, if you did any harm at all, write down that person's name. As in the Fourth Step, we're interested only in *our* part—in harm that *we* have done. Include institutions, too, such as a store you might have stolen from, a client you overbilled, or an insurance company you defrauded.

When I first tried making an Eighth Step list, I found it impossible to look at my entire life at once. I could grab only a name here, an incident there, an event from somewhere else. My life seemed too big, too amorphous, too hazy and disorganized for me to see it as clearly as I needed to. So I decided to break it into parts—periods that made internal sense to me and were more manageable. The first period covered the years I had been free of alcohol and drugs. There were five such years then, and they felt like a single piece. I searched slowly backward through them, writing down the name of each person whom it seemed to me I had harmed in some way, and a few words to indicate how.

The next period comprised the two years preceding that, dating back to the breakup of my marriage. I searched those years for people I had harmed, setting down their names. Then I moved backward again, through yet another two-year period, then through a nine-year period in which I had lived with my wife and children in the mountains . . . and so on.

Following the counsel in AA's book *Twelve Steps and Twelve Traditions* to "walk back through our lives as far as memory will reach," I brought my list back to the time I was eight or nine years old. My memory extended further, but younger than that I couldn't see that I had done much harm. In all, there were ten periods. I searched each of them.

Some of what I set down was grave and hurtful to remember. Some was more embarrassing than painful. Some encompassed incidents that other people might consider trivial but that had bothered me on some level for years. Here is an entry from my own list that refers to a harm I did by omission rather than commission, and not a very great one either:

"*Arabian Nights*—St. Viator's."

What the entry meant was this. Completing the eighth grade at St. Viator's elementary school in Chicago and graduating, I hadn't finished reading a copy of the *Arabian Nights* that I'd taken out from the school library. I was enraptured by the book. So I kept it, planning to read it over the summer and return it to the school in the fall. Summer was busy, fall came. I began my freshman year at a high school outside my neighborhood.

Two years later, my family moved. I still hadn't gotten around to reading the book, so I packed it up and took it with my other belongings out to Park Ridge, a suburb north and west of the city. And packed it up again and brought it up to college with me in Wisconsin two years later, still unread, with me feeling a little guilty and thinking that if I didn't read it soon, I'd have to send it back anyway. And packed it up again two years later and had it shipped to New York, when I left for a university there. . . .

And so it went, for thirty-four years.

I packed and unpacked that book, put it up on shelves, took it down, and put it up on yet new shelves again and again over three and a half decades and half the United States.

Now certainly Western civilization was not imperiled by my act. No one went mad, no one died; no one was made to weep inconsolably through the night. There was not, I think we would all agree, harm of an egregious nature here. Still, to my perception, I had done harm: I had taken something that was not mine. I had, for three and a half decades, deprived many young students of the pleasure of this book. So down it went on my Eighth Step list.

Not everything on the list was so light; some was excruciating, made me wince with pain. Did I do that? *Could* I have done that? Yes, I could. And had. It is in moments of such difficult recollection, and admission, that the value of simply sitting still, breathing in and breathing out, of following one's breath for a minute or two becomes apparent.

Make your Eighth Step list as long as it needs to be. If only half a dozen names should be on it, fine. If a hundred or even more should, that's also fine. What matters is that you be as honest as you can in determining what people or institutions you have harmed. Finish your list within three months after beginning it, six weeks if you can.

Becoming Willing

Once your list is finished, how do you go about accomplishing the second part of the Step: *and became willing to make amends to them all?*

To become willing is to become ready, disposed to; to accept that, sooner or later, you will. Willingness, in my case, was something that I sensed more than something I could measure. Being willing didn't necessarily mean that I *wanted* to make amends (though in many cases I discovered I did). Also, while I became willing to make some amends, I remained for a while unwilling to make others. Becoming willing was a process. It developed through my working the Steps, practicing the other parts of Prospering, meditation and prayer, and asking whatever I conceived of as a Higher Power to give it to me.

Use all of these in your own search for willingness, along with any other means you find effective. Keep in mind that willingness is not an all-or-nothing proposition here. To be willing to make some amends while still unwilling to make others, or to be more willing in a given case than not but still to feel some reluctance, is perfectly all right—and enough to begin moving into the Ninth Step.

Step Nine

"Made direct amends to such people wherever possible, except when to do so would injure them or others."

A lot of people balk at this Step or at the thought of making certain amends. That's natural. The Step threatens our ego, pride. It triggers a desire to justify ourselves.

The best way around this resistance is to advance into the Step gradually. Begin by going over your Eighth Step list with whomever you did your Fifth Step, or with someone else trustworthy and experienced with the Steps. This can give you a helpful perspective.

"Jerry," said the man with whom I went over my list, "it's 'made a list of all persons we had *harmed*,' not annoyed."

Through him I came to see that some of the harm I thought I'd done wasn't harm at all, but simply a breach of manners or adolescent callousness. I also gained a better understanding of some of the real harm I *had* caused. But most valuable, the simple act of sharing my list lessened the discomfort I felt over the prospect of making some of these amends.

Bob, the medical writer whom we met in Chapter 7, says, "I got a wholly unexpected benefit out of it too. The list, I realized, constituted for me a new Fourth Step. And by going over it with another person, I undertook another Fifth Step. It was a powerful experience for both of us."

How do we make amends? And what are "direct" amends?

The Latin *emendare*, from which the word *amends* derives, means "to free from fault." Amends, in its primary definition, means reparation—a repairing. To make amends is to set right what is wrong in the sense of broken or hurt: to repair something.

In practical terms, there are three basic ways we can go about doing that: by apologizing or expressing our regret; by restoring money or goods that we deprived the person of (or correcting damage we caused in other ways, such as to someone's reputation); and by making ongoing or living amends—doing what we can not to repeat this behavior and cause this kind of harm to anyone else.

Is it necessary to apologize to the person we actually harmed? Couldn't we just do what we can to remedy the situation and try not to repeat such actions? Maybe, I don't know. I *do* know that it's natural to wish to avoid a face-to-face meeting. To make amends in person, over the telephone, or even by letter is uncomfortable. The Step, however, says *direct amends*. This language is as open to interpretation as the language in any other Step, but *direct* means to me pretty much what the dictionary has it mean—straightforward, without any intervening conditions or agencies.

My experience and observation is that to make amends directly is the most powerful way, the most freeing and restorative of ourselves and of our relationships. Where possible, make your amends in person. If you can't, because of circumstances such as distance or potentially violent anger in the other party, then make amends by telephone or letter, whichever seems appropriate. Here, as an example of how you might phrase your amends, is one of my own, in letter form. Remember the copy of *Arabian Nights* that I took from my elementary school library? This is what I finally did.

30 December 1989

Sister Virginia Ann Fannin, Librarian*
St. Viator's School
4140 W. Addison Avenue
Chicago, Illinois 60641

Dear Sister Virginia Ann Fannin:

I graduated from St. Viator's elementary school in June of 1955. At that time, I had not yet finished reading a book, a version of the Arabian Nights, that I had checked out of the 8th-grade library and which I dearly loved and was hugely enjoying. So I took it home with me, intending to finish reading it over the summer and to get it back to St. Viator's in the fall.

Nearly 35 years have passed since then. Here, albeit severely overdue, is the book.

Not long ago I undertook a thorough inventory of my life and behavior to date, toward the goal of setting right as best I could all harms I had caused. One aspect of my behavior I noted, of which this book is an example, is that while I do not and have never considered myself a thief, there has been a pattern of "appropriations" in my life. I desire not to repeat this in the future, and to make amends for such incidents in the past.

So herewith, I return this book (which I had always planned to do, but which, over the decades, I never did) with my apologies to the school and to the many students who were deprived of the pleasure of it over the years. I'm enclosing also my check for $25,

---

* I called the school to determine whether or not it was still open, and the name of the current librarian.

*which I hope you will be able to use to buy books for the library.
And I hope that those books will give to your students the same
kind of pleasure the library's books gave to me when I was there.*

Thank you, and bless you.

> *Sincerely,*
> *Jerrold Mundis*

The elements in this amends are:

1. A simple statement of what I did
2. A statement of the process I'm engaged in and
   what I hope to accomplish through it*
3. An apology
4. Reparation (the return of the book)
5. An additional gesture of amends (the check),
   which was strictly a personal choice and which
   I made because it felt right

The first, third, and fourth of these elements, I think, are
appropriate to nearly every amends. For me, so is the second
(it deepens the process). At the very minimum, amends should
include an apology and reparation. If you plan to make
amends in person or over the telephone, you might want to
write out a brief script first, jot down some notes, or mentally
rehearse something close to what you intend to say. This will
make the actual amends easier to do.

Organize your Eighth Step list into three groups: amends
that will be fairly easy to make, amends of middle range, and
amends that will be difficult. Begin your Ninth Step work

---

* Some people make reference to the Steps or recovery when they make amends; I choose
not to. Others don't refer at all to the process they're involved in; I generally do.

with a middle-range amends—challenging enough to build some muscle (which will make subsequent amends easier) but not so much as to daunt you. (If you truly can't bring yourself to start with a middle-range amends, then start with an easy one.) I began by making amends over an incident involving a surreptitiously "borrowed" wool blanket in which there had been no serious harm but that nevertheless was embarrassing and hard on my ego. Go to a difficult one next. Then an easy one, and then a hard one. This schedule is a suggestion. In the end, make your amends in whatever rhythm and mix you can —any way is a good way.

Avoid writing a scenario in your mind as to how a particular amends will be received. Otherwise, you'll be more concerned with the effect of your amends than with making the amends. You might also be tempted to feel annoyed or disappointed if the other party doesn't respond the way you hoped or imagined she would. My part is simply to make the amends. How that is received is beyond my power to determine. (Generally the result is positive. Forgiveness takes place, reconciliations occur. Often both parties are freed of resentment. Most people will appreciate what you're doing; they may even express love, friendship, or gratitude. But that is not always the case. Some may be embarrassed, others angry; one or two might tell you to go jump in front of a train.) Regardless of the response, you'll find that you have emerged from the amends a freer person.

Be straightforward and sincere. If someone wants a pound of your flesh in addition to the amends you are making, you are under no obligation to deliver it. Nor, though, should you argue or try justify yourself. Just make your amends and accept that you are powerless over how they are received.

Cross out the names of those to whom you make amends as you work through your list. A Ninth Step might take several years to complete (yes, years), and as unlikely as it may seem at this point, you may even forget whether you have made amends to someone as time passes.

Sometimes a person on your list will loom up unexpectedly in your life. Startled, you might wonder: Is this the moment? Usually, the answer is yes. If it weren't, the question would probably not even occur to you. Everyone who works the Ninth Step will eventually have an anecdote or two about turning a corner in some foreign city or at an airport and running into someone on his list whom he hadn't seen in years.

At another time you might be with someone to whom you haven't yet felt ready to make amends, when, for some reason, the impulse will come to you. Again, it's usually appropriate to go ahead.

"This happened to me with my youngest son," said Tim, a financial planner.* "He was twenty at the time. The harm I'd caused him—which had never been intentional but which was harm nonetheless; the pain he'd suffered because of the divorce, and other reasons—was a source of tremendous grief to me. I was working up to this amends, had planned to do it in the fall, some four or five months off. But here we were in my apartment, talking happily, enjoying each other, and the thought burst into my consciousness: *Now?*

"Fear hit me. It almost took my breath away. But I knew it was time. I swallowed, breathed, and said softly, 'Andy, there's something I'd like to talk with you about. . . .'

"It was the right time."

It nearly always is.

How do you make amends to someone who is now dead or to someone from long ago whom it is impossible to find? Write a letter to her—an actual letter. Talk to her, review the

---

* I have known several underearners who worked in financial areas or held MBAs, even one who taught at a prestigious business school. No one is immune to underearning.

harm you did, tell her what this process is about, and make your apology. Sign the letter with your first name. Fold it and put it in an envelope. Write the name of the person on the outside and the name of the city you most closely associate with her—nothing more. Put a stamp on the envelope. Drop the envelope into a mailbox. And as you do, feel in your heart the amends you are making; then turn the rest over to the care of the universe.

When there is also restitution to be made in such a case—say, repayment of a loan or return of property—you can make the restitution symbolically. Donate, in that person's name, whatever sum of money is involved to an appropriate organization or charity. Carl, a medical technician, had been addicted to chocolate when he was a child and had stolen great numbers of chocolate bars from mom-and-pop grocery stores in the early 1950s. These stores had long since disappeared. To make restitution, he bought $300 worth of chocolate and donated it to a foster-children program. Erin, who manages a photocopy shop, had failed to return a roommate's share of a security deposit on a house that they and others had briefly rented together. The woman had since moved out of state. Erin was unable to locate her. So she donated the $210 she had appropriated from this woman to a shelter for the homeless and sent a brief expression of regret over what she'd done along with it.

There is a caveat in the Ninth Step: Do not make direct amends, it says, when to do so would injure the person to whom we are making amends or someone else. This danger might arise when making direct amends would mean involving someone else who participated with us in doing the harm. Here, we have no right to reveal his role or implicate him. Another example might be when to make direct amends would deeply hurt the person we had harmed, who till now had been unaware of our role. In such cases we can, however—and it is to our benefit to do so—make *indirect* amends. We can do this by repairing any damage we can and then by trying to live in a way that won't cause that kind of harm again. There are few situations in which it is best for us not to make direct amends. Be sure you aren't telling yourself that *this*—whatever it is—is one of them simply because you want to avoid making the amends. If you're legitimately uncertain, talk the question over with the person with whom you shared your Eighth Step list.

Break the ice with this Step by committing yourself to make your first amends within ten days after you go over your Eighth Step list with someone else.

Step Ten

"Continued to take personal inventory and when we were wrong promptly admitted it."

The Tenth Step has to do with the present. The past is over; you've made peace with it through the Eighth and Ninth Steps. The Tenth Step helps you live more effectively and pleasurably in today.

Many of us have trouble admitting it when we're wrong, especially when we aren't accustomed to doing so. It feels like being put in the inferior position or being criticized.

To be wrong, for our purposes, is to act primarily out of character defects: envy, pride, self-pity, and the like. The question relates just as much to how we feel or act when we're alone as it does to how we deal with others.

When you find yourself growing fearful, angry, or agitated in some manner, take a moment to run a quick inventory on yourself: What's being threatened in you? Your self-esteem, a personal relationship? Your security, your sex life, your ambition? To recognize this and admit it to yourself is to do the Tenth Step. I do more of my own Tenth Step work this way than in admitting to *others* that I am wrong—for the simple reason that recognizing and admitting to myself that I am, or even that I *may* be wrong, often gives me the perspective to alter my behavior before I behave poorly toward someone else.

Often. Not always.

Sometimes I do not even think of the Tenth Step or any other tool in this book until it's too late. Then, as best I can, I try to admit that I was wrong and to express my regret. That has always been a cleansing thing to do.

Another good way to work the Tenth Step is to take a few minutes before you go to sleep to review the day. Is there anything you regret having done? Did you cause harm anywhere? If so, you'll probably want to apologize. In time, or maybe even shortly, there will be fewer such events in your days.

I want to make a strong suggestion here:

I suggest that you begin immediately to do a Tenth Step every night specifically on underearning.

This is a simple, powerful way to work the Tenth Step directly on your underearning. Here's how to do it:

First, review your activities of the day against the Three Do-Nots of Prospering:

1. Did you incur a new debt today?
2. Did you accept work that pays you less than you need?
3. Did you turn down money?

If your answer to any of these is yes, you need to be aware of that. Because if you continue such behavior, the chances that you will ever free yourself from underearning are slim.

Second, check your activities for other forms of underearning. Did you quote too low a price for a job, spend more time on a project than you're being paid to, put off again any thought of asking for a raise? These are less serious than any of the Three Do-Nots, but unchecked and in accumulation they will still make your liberation from underearning much more difficult in the long run. Few practices will make you as quickly and vividly aware of your tendency, or disposition, or compulsion to underearn as this one will.

When you do find examples in your day, don't be critical of yourself—simply recognize them for what they are, and use that recognition to inform yourself when you make choices and take actions in the days to come.

The first month I used this way of doing the Tenth Step was a revelation. I found myself nearly on a daily basis negotiating doggedly for less than I needed, turning down money, spending time on projects and busywork that would bring in little or no income, and underearning in other ways. Three years later, I am still amazed on occasion, when I return to this practice after a period of neglect, to discover that I have been drifting back unawares toward the same place again.

Maintain a steady involvement with the Tenth Step.

Step Eleven

"Sought through prayer and meditation to improve our conscious contact with God <u>as we understood Him</u>, praying only for a knowledge of His will for us and the power to carry that out."

When, after long resistance, I finally began to work with this Step, I replaced the comma with a period, ending it after the first clause: "Sought through prayer and meditation to improve our conscious contact with God <u>as we understood Him</u>."

Period.

That was the only way I could even hope to engage with the Step. I found the second part almost incomprehensible. What it suggested—an utter surrender of my own will, of my own wishes and desires—was terrifying. It was depressing, enraging. I wanted nothing to do with it.

So with what grasp I had of prayer and meditation then, I began to seek to improve my conscious contact with God as I understood God. I did so tentatively, mistrustfully.

I took *seeking* to mean intent: what I wanted, was looking for. To *improve* I saw as to increase, or make clearer. *Conscious contact* I took to mean discovery, a coming together, a being with or of.

And indeed that was what came about, in ways that were sometimes subtle and at other times more obvious. As time passed, I moved more deeply into meditation and prayer, my conscious contact or awareness increased, and each enhanced and expanded the other. In one of AA's books, in a chapter on the Eleventh Step, is a sentence that, slightly altered, reads: "Those of us who have come to make regular use of prayer and meditation would no more do without them than we would refuse air, food, or sunshine."

That is true for me.

We've already discussed prayer and meditation in the manner I think best suited to this book. You'll find any further exploration into them pleasurable and rich.

Let's move on to the second part of the Step, then, the part I so detested at first (as have many others). My own early experience with God, or with the God of my childhood religion, was, as cited earlier, brutal: That God was brutal, his will was brutal. The emotions that result from such an experience don't die easily, even when the intellect has come to know better. I had to work hard to become able even to begin to consider the second part of the Step: *praying only for a knowledge of His will for us and the power to carry that out.*

The concept made me sick. Every cell in my body recoiled in disgust. I had to reassure myself by repeatedly summoning up memories of the positive experiences I'd had with the other Steps, with prayer and meditation, and with the conscious contact I had known. I needed to know viscerally as well as intellectually that it was God *as I understood God* whose will I desired to know and carry out, not the God of my childhood.

The Step could read, for example, if I wished it to: "Sought through prayer and meditation to improve our conscious contact with what was best in us and best in other people, praying only for a knowledge of its will for us and the power to carry that out."

I could do that. I could pray only for a knowledge of the will of what was best in me and best in other people and the power to carry that out.

The fear I had of this Step, and the fear of practically anyone who's ever been reluctant to approach it, was that God's will would not be consonant with my own. In other words, that I wouldn't get what I want. It is very difficult to pray only for a knowledge of God's will for you and the power to carry that out when you fear that this might mean something you don't want: suffering, being hurt, being deprived, punished, not getting what you want or think you need.

But it's not difficult to pray only for a knowledge of the will of what is best in you and best in other people and the power to carry that out. Take a moment to sit quietly and identify what is truly best in you and in the people you know.

Do it now. (Spend only a minute or two; there's no need to be comprehensive.)

Finished? Good.

Most of us would be willing to accept what that best—in ourselves and others—would desire for us, and most of us would be grateful for the power to bring it about: not only in matters relating to money and earning but in others too. (And the fact is, the more broadly you apply the Eleventh Step across the spectrum of your life, the greater will be its impact on your earning.)

I am, anyway.

There is another practice I follow in the context of this Step, which I recommend to you. To the best of my ability, I try not to attach my sense of happiness or well-being to the having of any person, place, or thing. I try to look within myself for that. I *do* want certain people, places, and things. And I make plans for how I might bring them into my life, and I work to do so. But I do not make my happiness or sense of well-being conditional upon having them. If I *were* to—if, say, I made my happiness or sense of well-being dependent upon the having of external things like money, fame, a spouse, an apartment—then I must *a priori* be miserable if I do not have them and be in constant, urgent, and desperate pursuit of them: because I cannot be happy or whole without them. And if I do get them, then I must begin to spend time and energy defending them, so they won't be taken from me, and controlling them, so they won't leave me, and live in terror lest I lose them—because I need them in order to be happy and whole, and that means that if I do lose them, I will be empty and hollow and miserable once again.

So, while I definitely have preferences and hopes and desires, I do my best not to make my happiness or sense of well-being conditional on the getting or fulfilling of any of them.

There is an additional consideration in this question of desire, or self-will, and that is this: There are times when what we want—though we think it will heal us and finally make us

complete and content—is actually not at all in our best interests. Nearly all of us have had the experience of intensely,
burningly wanting someone or something, and striving might-
ily to gain that person or thing, and finally succeeding, only
later to have it blow up on us and inflict grievous harm and
pain upon us. Though I think I'm much better at knowing
what is best for me these days than I once was, I can still be
mistaken. My will, as opposed, say, to the will of what is best
in me and best in other people, can cause me harm. So it
seems to me sensible to do what I can to be as open and
inviting as I can to the will of a Higher Power as I understand
it.

I'd like to close with a story I've always liked, which
speaks to me of will and desire, of getting what *I* want, and as
I want it, and of trust:

Just above a mountain valley stood a great dam. The
dam began to crack, soon to give way completely, and water began to roar down into the valley. A National Guard
unit was rushed in to evacuate the valley's residents.

The water was already several feet high and rising. The
first guardsmen were working from rubber rafts. One
raftful came upon a house where a man was sitting on the
sill of a second-floor window, the water swirling just below
his feet.

"Hurry up!" yelled a guardsman. "Get in! The whole
valley's going under in four minutes!"

With a serene smile, the man waved them off. "No. Go
away," he said. "I put all my trust in the Lord."

The guardsmen left to help others.

Two minutes later, another group came by in a power-
boat. The man was now standing on his roof, the water
lapping at his shoes. "Come on, get in!" a guardsman
shouted. "The valley's going under in two minutes!"

The man shook his head. "No. Go away," he said. "I put all my trust in the Lord."

The guardsmen left.

Two minutes later, another group returned in a helicopter. By now, the man was standing on his chimney, the water rising up over his ankles. A guardsman tossed out a rope ladder from the helicopter. "Hurry up!" he shouted. "Grab the ladder! The valley's going under in seconds!"

"No! Go away," the man shouted back. "I put all my trust in the Lord!"

The helicopter left. . . .

A few minutes later, the man woke up in Heaven, just outside the Pearly Gates. "What happened!" he demanded angrily of God. "I put all my trust in you!"

God shrugged. "I sent you a raft, I sent you boat, I sent you a helicopter. What do you want?"

I do like that story. Now and then, when—despite all my fine character, excellent prayer and meditation, and clear and tireless actions—I'm still not getting what I want, I need to stop and take another, good, slow look around.

Step Twelve

"Having had a spiritual awakening as the result of these steps, we tried to carry this message to underearners, and to practice these principles in all our affairs."

This is the last of the Twelve Steps. What it says is that if I work the other Steps, I will undergo a spiritual awakening, some sort of change in my consciousness, gain some new awareness. This has been my experience. It has also, from what

I have been able to see, been the experience of other people who have engaged with them.

The Step then suggests that out of this new awareness or consciousness, I try to carry this message—the message that change is possible, that freedom from underearning, a new life, is possible—to other underearners. The most elemental way for anyone to do this is simply by getting free of underearning himself or herself, to serve as an example just by living this new life.

Do not proselytize or go dashing about actively trying to save other underearners. It won't work, and you'll only annoy people or trigger their denial. Freedom from underearning, as we said earlier, is not for people who need it; it's for people who want it. What you *can* do is be willing to share your experience, strength, and hope with anyone who is in pain over this condition and whom you think might be helped by your doing so. You might give him or her a copy of this book. You might found a meeting where you can help yourself and others to become free and stay free. Do whatever seems right to you.

My own experience is that when I try to carry this message to other underearners, I strengthen and make richer my own recovery, my own liberation from underearning.

Finally, the Twelfth Step suggests that I practice these principles, the principles embodied in the Steps, in all my affairs. Not just around the issue of underearning, but in every aspect of my life. Not perfectly, but as I can.

And again, my experience with this part of the Step is that when I do, I prosper: that my life is good, and I enjoy my life, and I like *being* alive—even when, as at times it will be, that is hard.

Those times do not seem to matter much.

I've been more directive in these two chapters on the Twelve Steps than ideally I would prefer. The Steps are personal. There is no one way to work them. I have been this directive in order to make them accessible to people who've never encountered them before and to provide clear ways to work with them; also, to suggest to those people who *are* familiar with them, but in another context, how they can be used in regard to earning—something about which many have expressed confusion at first.

Follow these pathways into the territory. Then blaze trails of your own—gloriously, and as you will.

10.

SUMMING UP

This brings Prospering to a close.

Prospering is a living program, not a theory. It works to the degree that you are willing to work it. This book won't do you much good if it's gathering dust on a shelf. Use it. Work with it. Integrate its material into your life on a daily basis. The more you do, the better off you'll be. If you practice its techniques and absorb its concepts, you *will* free yourself from underearning, you *will* stay free, and you *will* go on to live prosperously, in a state of thriving, of steady improvement, and to know abundance, to have all that you need in ample supply.

The practical elements of Prospering—not incurring new debt, raising fees, diversifying—are important, even essential, and will have immediate positive impact on your earning. The spiritual or psychological elements—meditation, Having Tea with Your Emotions, working the Steps—while of less immediate impact, are equally important. Ultimately, *they* are what will effect the deep inner change, the fundamental shift in your attitudes and perceptions about money, yourself, and yourself in relationship to money, that is necessary if your freedom from underearning is to be lasting.

The practical and the spiritual strengthen one another. Each is integral to Prospering. Together, they form the whole. Indeed, as you practice them, the divisions between them begin to dissolve, and there is only *prospering*—a way of life.

I do not mean for you to work this program in a mechanical way, or to overwhelm yourself by trying to implement all of its parts at once or even, possibly, ever. Freedom from underearning is a path, a way, a creative process: You will make discoveries of your own and come to work Prospering in the manner that is best suited to you.

Still, certain practices are fundamental. As a simple core, follow these ten guidelines:

Core

1. Observe carefully the Three Do-Nots:

    * Do not incur any new debt.
    * Do not take work that pays you less than you need.
    * Do not say no to money.

2. Each night, mentally check your day against what you know of underearning, to see if you have been engaged in it.
3. Keep a Spending Record.
4. Create a Spending Plan.
5. List three practical actions from Chapter 5 (and from Chapter 6 if it is relevant) that would have positive impact on your earning, and take them.

6. List the three psychological or spiritual prac-
    tices from Chapter 7 that you find the most
    appealing, and begin to practice them.
7. Review the two lists above at intervals, adding
    and subtracting items according to your
    changing situation.
8. Establish a support group, even if that's only
    two or three people, and meet with them for
    an hour on a regular basis.
9. Remain open to other concepts and techniques
    that you can integrate into Prospering that
    will help you.
10. Work, or at the very least consider working,
    the Twelve Steps.

From there, the next movements will be apparent.

A CLOSING NOTE

You do not have to underearn. You can free yourself from the
tendency, habit, or compulsion to do so and remain free of it
forever. You have already begun, by reading this book. If you
integrate its concepts into your life and practice its techniques,
one day at a time, you are bound to be successful.

I wish you a life of prosperity and abundance. . . .

APPENDIX A

SECURED DEBT, UNSECURED DEBT*

What is debt?

In its simplest definition, you are in debt when you owe some person or institution money. We need a refinement, though. For our purposes, a secured loan is not a debt, even though money has been loaned to you.

SECURED DEBT

To secure something is to make it safe. When you secure a loan, you free the lender from any risk of losing his money. That's why he's willing to lend it to you—he has no fear of loss.

Your word, your good faith, even your unfailing history of

---

* Adapted from the author's book *How to Get Out of Debt, Stay Out of Debt & Live Prosperously.*

repayment do not secure a loan. What happens if you have a medical emergency, lose your job, or simply go bonkers and run off to Brazil—if, for *any* reason, you just don't have the money to pay the loan back? The lender loses his money, that's what.

Collateral, in its primary definition, is something that runs side by side with something else. In financial terms, collateral is property you pledge to the lender or actually give to him to hold during the course of the loan. That property is security; it's what makes the lender's money safe or secured. When you pay him back, he returns it to you.

A loan from a pawnshop is a classic example. You bring your camera to the pawnbroker. He lends you $50. When you repay him the $50 (plus interest, of course), he gives your camera back to you. If you don't repay him, he keeps your camera. You don't own your camera anymore, but you don't owe him $50 either. The loan is over.

Fine, you say, but *you're* not interested in hockshops and cameras. You're talking *big* money—$5,000, $50,000, more.

The numbers don't make any difference: A loan is a loan, whether it's for $5, $500, or $50,000. And collateral is collateral, whether it's a television set or a television station.

One of the most common forms of secured loan is a mortgage. Let's say I'm buying a house for $100,000. I've saved $20,000, which I use for the down payment. The bank likes my job history, my salary, and my credit record. They have confidence in me. But that confidence alone isn't enough to persuade them to lend me the additional $80,000 I need, not without strings attached. Life's too unpredictable for that. So they require me to give them a mortgage on my house—a document that generally grants them all legal rights to it if I default, that is, if I fail to make my loan payments for a specified period of time, usually about four months. The bank then has the right to foreclose the mortgage, to take possession of my house in lieu of what I owe them, sell it, and keep the proceeds or the bulk of the proceeds for themselves, thus recouping their $80,000. I've secured the loan by pledging my house as collateral. I've eliminated the risk that the bank will lose their money if they lend it to me.

Car loans work the same way. I buy a new Chevy for $12,000. I put $4,000 of my own money down and borrow the balance, $8,000, from a bank or from General Motors. To get the financing, I sign a document that gives the lender all rights and title to the car if I don't pay the loan back.

If I default in either of these cases, I lose my house or my car. That would be painful, but I would not owe money to anyone. I would not go into debt.*

A cash loan can also be secured. Of course, the collateral has to be worth at least as much—and usually more—than the amount borrowed. No bank will accept $1,000 worth of stock certificates as collateral against a $5,000 loan, just as no pawnbroker will lend me $25 if I give him my Bic lighter to hold.

These are examples of collateral often used to secure cash loans:

- Bearer bonds
- Stock certificates
- Home equity, in the form of a second mortgage
- Parcels of land or other real estate
- Inventory
- Works of art
- Whole life insurance policies
- Precious metals
- An owned franchise

---

* Be careful about this when buying a car. Pay a large amount down, enough so that the value of the car, if you had to sell it or turn it over to the bank, would be greater than the amount you still owe on it.

- Copyrights
- Patents
- A business

As anyone who's in debt knows very well, banks and financial institutions aren't the only places we can get a loan. We borrow from employers in the form of salary advances, from the government, from colleges and universities for educational loans, from business associates, from acquaintances and co-workers, from friends and relatives.

The most frequent loan in America is probably the one taken from a friend:

"Can you let me have five dollars till tomorrow?"

"I need twenty dollars till payday."

"Can you spare three hundred dollars till my commission check comes in?"

"My broker's check won't reach me for another week. Can you spot me fifteen hundred dollars till then?"

The loan from family members is also common. Young couples setting up household or buying their first house frequently borrow from their families. I bought my own first house in 1971. Everything I'd saved went for the down payment and closing costs. There were several other expenses involved in moving my family from a city apartment to a house in the mountains, so I borrowed $7,500 from my father.

Houses, of course, aren't the only things for which we tap relatives. We borrow from them when we're between jobs, for education, vacations, Christmas buying, for furniture, medical expenses, big tax bills, births, marriages, divorces, to get over a hump, or when things are difficult in general.

These loans are usually given on good faith alone; but occasionally they're secured too. There's even more latitude in finding collateral for a personal loan than there is for a commercial loan. Commercial lenders want collateral for which there's a ready market and a constant demand, which assures them they can convert it to cash immediately if the borrower defaults. While friends or relatives might eventually prefer to do the same thing, they're usually satisfied with collateral in the form of something they'd like to own or use themselves, such as a camcorder. As collateral on a $2,500 loan, I once offered a friend an antique ivory statue he'd always admired.

The possibilities for collateral on personal loans are nearly limitless. For example, you can use:

- Anything that could secure a commercial loan
- A VCR
- A piece of jewelry
- A fur coat
- A work of art
- A musical instrument
- An antique
- A computer
- A coin collection
- A set of encyclopedias
- A sewing machine
- Luggage
- Furniture
- A camera
- A snowmobile
- A power tool
- A rug

To sum it up, a secured loan is this: Someone lends you money, you give him an article of equivalent or greater value to hold until you pay him back.

WHY SECURED LOANS ARE NOT DEBT

From a strict point of view, a secured loan *is* debt: It's money you "owe." But there is a difference, and that difference is *crucial*.

If things go wrong, for any reason at all, and you can't repay the loan, what happens? You forfeit your property. That may be painful, but *you are not obligated to pay money to anyone*.

You walk away clean. You don't owe anyone money. You're not in debt.

UNSECURED DEBT
(THIS IS IT)

Unsecured debt is:

1. Any amount of cash you borrow without putting up collateral
2. Any credit extended to you
3. Any service you take without paying for at the moment you receive it

Some common examples of incurring unsecured debt are:

- You're short this week, so you tap a friend at the office for $20.
- You need $500 to tide you over for a month, so you borrow it from your bank on your signature alone.
- You need a new winter coat but you don't have the money, so you call your parents and borrow it from them.

- You're out with a friend, you want to pick something up from a store, but you don't have enough cash, so you borrow a few dollars from him.
- You need your tax refund now and can't wait for it to arrive, so you ask your brother for $300.
- You buy a compact disc player from Macy's and charge it to your account.
- You gas up your car on your Mobil card.
- You go out to dinner and hand the waiter your Visa card.
- You fly to Chicago to spend Thanksgiving with your relatives and put the tickets on your American Airlines card.
- You buy your spring wardrobe on your Bloomingdale's card.
- You charge a new lawn mower to your Sears account.
- You need your car fixed, but you can't pay your mechanic till next month; that's fine with him, so he does the work.
- Your child's college tuition is due, so you request an advance on salary or commissions.
- You need two caps and a root canal but you don't have the money, so you arrange with your dentist to pay her off over the next several months.

These are all actual, unsecured debts. You owe money to these people. They have no collateral from you: Your dentist can't sell the plaster cast of your mouth, Sears can't convert your signature into cash.

THIS IS IT TOO

But we're not finished yet. There are other, more subtle ways to incur unsecured debt. What happens when you get behind on your rent?

My rent is $1,100 per month. Let's say it's July now. And let's say that last month I finally went for the eye exam I'd been putting off. It had been three years, and my ophthalmologist wanted to do a full scan, which was sensible. My eyes proved healthy, but I did need a new prescription. The exam was $175, two new pairs of glasses $300. My television, possibly in a gesture of sympathy with my old glasses, decided to commit suicide at the same time. So I bought a new one for $400. And since I don't usually keep such things in mind, I was unhappily surprised to find that the premium for my life insurance was due, for $200. That's $1,075 I hadn't planned on spending in June.

Money's tight. So I don't pay my rent in July, planning to catch up in August. What I've done is taken a service—the use of my apartment—without paying for it.

I owe money; I've incurred a debt.

Could I have paid my rent? Sure. I might have arranged with my ophthalmologist to pay him off over a couple of months, bought my glasses on an American Express card, and put the television on Visa.

Either way, I go into debt.

Falling behind on unsecured obligations, then, is the second category of debt. The most common areas in which we do this are:

- Rent
- Telephone service
- Utilities (gas, electricity, water)
- Federal, state, and local income taxes

- Property taxes
- Alimony and child support
- Tuition
- Fuel bills

Surprising just how many ways there are to go into debt, isn't it? There's a whole supermarket of opportunities out there. Debt, then, comes in almost limitless variations, but it's not hard to recognize once we're clear on what it is—borrowing cash without collateral, buying goods or taking services without paying for them immediately, and falling behind in unsecured obligations. That recognition is a good start.

APPENDIX B

THE TWELVE STEPS OF ALCOHOLICS ANONYMOUS

Step One

We admitted we were powerless over alcohol—that our lives had become unmanageable.

Step Two

Came to believe that a Power greater than ourselves could restore us to sanity.

Step Three

Made a decision to turn our will and our lives over to the care of God <u>as we understood Him</u>.

Step Four

Made a searching and fearless moral inventory of ourselves.

Step Five

Admitted to God, to ourselves, and to another human being the exact nature of our wrongs.

Step Six

Were entirely ready to have God remove all these defects of character.

Step Seven

Humbly asked Him to remove our shortcomings.

Step Eight

Made a list of all persons we had harmed, and became willing to make amends to them all.

Step Nine

Made direct amends to such people wherever possible, except when to do so would injure them or others.

Step Ten

Continued to take personal inventory and when we were wrong promptly admitted it.

Step Eleven

Sought through prayer and meditation to improve our conscious contact with God <u>as we understood Him</u>, praying only for a knowledge of His will for us and the power to carry that out.

Step Twelve

Having had a spiritual awakening as a result of these steps, we tried to carry this message to alcoholics, and to practice these principles in all our affairs.

These Steps and ways to work with them to help free yourself from underearning are discussed in Chapters 8 and 9. The word *underearning* is substituted for *alcohol* there.

FOR FURTHER
READING

There are many books of many kinds that can help you in your liberation from underearning. This short list reflects titles that I think will cover the most ground in the most effective way for the largest number of readers. Use them as a jumping-off point.

Alcoholics Anonymous (New York: Alcoholics Anonymous World Services, 1939). The basic handbook of AA. A thorough, insightful treatment of compulsive behavior, specifically alcoholism. Contains AA's recovery program. Many people have found this program valuable for freeing themselves from other kinds of self-damaging behavior as well.

Feeling Good: The New Mood Therapy by David Burns, M.D. (New York: William Morrow, 1980). A fine exposition of cognitive psychology, which concerns itself with dysfunctional attitudes and perceptions that result in self-crippling depression and anxiety. Offers effective techniques for reworking these into realistic and beneficial ones.

How to Get Out of Debt, Stay Out of Debt & Live Prosperously by Jerrold Mundis (New York: Bantam Books, 1988). A complete and detailed program for doing precisely what the title says. Obviously I can't help but be biased here. Still, if you read only one book from this list, make it this one.

Investing for Safety's Sake by Michael D. Joehnk (New York: Harper & Row, 1988). How to put your savings to work for you in a safe and effective manner. Sometimes slow going, but clear and sound. A good, useful primer.

The Miracle of Mindfulness (revised edition) by Thich Nhat Hanh (Boston: Beacon Press, 1975). Simple, beautiful, lucid treatment of mindfulness, a form of meditation. Anything by Thich Nhat Hanh, a Vietnamese Zen master, is worth reading.

Money and the Meaning of Life by Jacob Needleman (New York: Doubleday, 1991). Needleman, a philosopher and professor of comparative religion, contends that the primary problem with money is not that we take it too seriously, but that we don't take it seriously *enough*. Man, he says, is unlikely to be successful in a spiritual quest unless he can deal effectively with the fundamental issue of money, which has come to contain practically the whole of human activity. Insightful, wise.

Money Is My Friend by Phil Laut (Cincinnati, OH: Trinity Publications, 1978). A small, extremely positive book that concentrates on the psychological elements of making money. Also contains some good practical suggestions on money management.

Money Troubles by Robin Leonard (Berkeley, CA: Nolo Press, 1991). Legal strategies for coping with debts of various kinds, from student loans to alimony. Leonard is an attorney. Good short-term, nuts-and-bolts material.

One Minute Wisdom by Anthony de Mello (New York: Image Books, 1985). Unfortunate title; superb anthology. Small parables/lessons drawn from the mystical traditions of East and West. The Master in these little tales is not one but many: a Hindu guru, a Zen roshi, a Taoist sage, a Jewish rabbi, a Christian monk, and a Sufi mystic. Anything by de Mello, an East Indian Jesuit and spiritual director, is worth reading.

The New Three Minute Meditator by David Harp (Oakland, CA: New Harbinger Publications, 1990). Lighthearted, easy, yet knowledgeable. A good, basic introduction to meditation.

The Richest Man in Babylon by George Clason (New York: Hawthorn Books, 1955). A slim volume on personal finance presented in the style of parables. Clear, sound, comprehensive treatment of basic principles.

Sylvia Porter's New Money Book for the 80's by Sylvia Porter (New York: Doubleday, 1975). A broad general survey of personal finance that covers just about every aspect you can think of. Some of the material is now dated, but most is still valid; a treasure-house of information and suggestions.

Smart Money (revised edition) by Ken and Daria Dolan (New York: Berkley Books, 1990). Personal banking, home buying, insurance, taxes, retirement plans, and similar topics. Each is covered in a single chapter presented in the form of common questions, with short, simple answers. Inclusive, reliable.

Twelve Steps and Twelve Traditions (New York: Alcoholics Anonymous World Services, 1953). Short, informing essays on the Steps and ways to work with them, in AA's traditional manner. Also contains essays on the Traditions, which are general guidelines for AA groups.

When Money Is the Drug by Donna Boundy (San Francisco: Harper San Francisco, 1993). Innovative, shrewd. Boundy names and explores a handful of strikingly common disorders about money. She understands how to have a healthy relationship with it.

ABOUT THE AUTHOR

Jerrold Mundis is a novelist and nonfiction writer. His short work has appeared in *The New York Times Magazine*, *American Heritage*, *Harper's Weekly*, and many other national magazines. A recovered underearner himself, he is the author of the best-selling *How to Get Out of Debt, Stay Out of Debt & Live Prosperously*.